find your
dream job

A PRACTICAL GUIDE TO
GETTING THE JOB YOU WANT

DENISE TAYLOR

This edition published in the UK in 2019 by Icon Books Ltd, Omnibus Business Centre, 39–41 North Road, London N7 9DP email: info@iconbooks.net www.iconbooks.net

Distributed in Australia and New Zealand by Allen & Unwin Pty Ltd, PO Box 8500, 83 Alexander Street, Crows Nest, NSW 2065

First published in the UK in 2013 by Icon Books

Distributed in Canada by Publishers Group Canada, 76 Stafford Street, Unit 300 Toronto, Ontario M6J 2S1

Sold in the UK, Europe and Asia by Faber & Faber Ltd, Bloomsbury House, 74–77 Great Russell Street, London WC1B 3DA or their agents

Distributed in the USA by Publishers Group West, 1700 Fourth Street, Berkeley, CA 94710

Distributed in South Africa by Jonathan Ball, Office B4, The District, 41 Sir Lowry Road, Woodstock 7925

ISBN: 978-178578-465-1

Typeset in Avenir by Marie Doherty

Printed and bound in Great Britain by Clays Ltd, Elcograf S.p.A.

About the author

One of the UK's top career strategists, **Denise Taylor** is an Award-Winning Career Coach, Chartered Psychologist, Associate Fellow of the British Psychological Society and a Registered Career Development Professional. Her books include *Now You've Been Shortlisted* and *Find Work at 50+*. Denise regularly appears as an expert at career forums, on radio and in the British press, including *The Times*, the *Sun*, *Esquire*, *Metro*, the *Daily Mail* and the *Guardian*.

Outside of work Denise loves adventurous travel, live music and living life to the full. We only have one life – make it a life you love.

Get access to How to Find a Job You Love, an eight-day programme by signing up via: www.subscribe page.com/t5y3j0

Over 50 – www.the50pluscoach.co.uk/sign-up/
www.denisetaylor.co.uk
www.amazingpeople.co.uk
Twitter – @amazingpeople
Facebook – www.facebook.com/amazingpeopleUK

Contents

1. Introduction

Why do some people find it easy to get the career move they want while others flounder and give up? A lot of it is down to what goes on inside their heads: when people think they will be successful, they probably will; but if they doubt themselves, their likelihood of success is slim.

I'm going to talk you through a process to ensure you stand the very best chance of success in getting the career you want. As a psychologist, I'll be including relevant and helpful psychological theory, but only when it makes a difference.

This book is full of practical advice, helpful tips and facts. It's also easy to read and focused on helping you to achieve your goals.

I want you to be a HERO to achieve your goals. I was introduced to the HERO concept by Professor Fred Luthans, University and George Holmes Distinguished Professor of Management at the University of Nebraska–Lincoln whose current research focuses on positive psychology. Being a HERO involves:

- **Hope** – that you will be successful and persevere as you work towards a goal.

- **Efficacy** – the self-confidence and the belief that you will succeed, and that you will put in the necessary effort.

- **Resilience** – to bounce back from disappointments and problems.

- **Optimism** – a positive mindset that you will succeed both now and in the future.

Without the belief that you can achieve your goal you may as well not even get started. But it can't be just a dream or a goal without foundation; you have to be willing to put in the work and to have sufficient background and experience to make you a credible candidate. This may mean that you need to choose an interim step, to find a job that will get you on the way to where you want to go.

We all have disappointments: we don't win the race, we lose out on buying something at an auction, or we have an injury that stops us participating in a game. It's how we respond to that disappointment that matters.

We have to treat each disappointment as a learning experience, and use this to do better next time. We also need to remember that sometimes the decision is outside our control. Just like an actor going for a casting call where the casting director may have an ideal in mind (if we are the wrong build or without a particular background, we will never be chosen), so at interview, the job may already be allocated to someone and the company is 'going through the motions', or they want someone with specific experience which wasn't made clear in the job ad.

Let's look at the process you will follow.

Be clear on your goal

You should be very clear on the job you are looking for, both the job title and your ideal company. Knowing the job provides focus for all further activity.

If you want to start a career, for example marketing in the fashion business, any activity you undertake from now on should be to enhance your chance of success and look good on your CV. If you want to move from management accountant to financial controller, your activity should focus on developing more senior leadership and business skills and experience to enhance your technical experience.

As a recent graduate you may have a desired goal, but in the short term be happy to be offered any job that seems like a step in the right direction.

Do you know what you want to do? If not, take time to do research to identify a career that will both excite you but that is also within your capability of getting. Chapter 2 will get you started.

Understand your target

Once you know the type of work you want and the type of organization you want to work for, you focus on research. Treat this like a research project and find out as much as possible about the organization, its competitors and the industry as a whole. This is covered in Chapter 3.

Building relationships through networking

You will probably find your next job through someone you know, so you need to network. Let me show you how to do this effectively in Chapter 4. I'll cover online networking too.

Fact-finding interviews

Sometimes you need to find out more about a job so you know whether you should apply or not. Setting up fact-finding interviews can really help your research phase, and sometimes lead to work. Chapter 5 will guide you in how to do this.

Understand your strengths to create your CV

You are not creating a CV in isolation; you should focus it on the particular job you seek. You must understand and be ready to exploit your strengths and your CV should make it clear to the reader what you want. Chapter 6 will focus on your CV.

Getting ready for your job search

We're going to take a time out before you get on to your job search proper. Having done all your preparation, what is the best strategy to take? You must be organized, and have some systems in place. We will cover this in Chapter 7.

Creating your message – the 'pitch'

You will need to develop a short 'pitch' you can say to anyone who asks what you are looking for. Too many do this badly; you'll be fine if you follow the guidance in Chapter 8.

LinkedIn

Facebook, LinkedIn, Pinterest ... where do you start? You probably use Facebook socially, so should you use this or something else to help you get a job? Right now you need an effective LinkedIn profile, and Chapter 9 will make sure you are using LinkedIn to your advantage.

Making applications

The most obvious way to get a job is to apply to job ads and upload your CV to job sites. Chapter 10 will make sure you follow sound advice to increase your chances of getting shortlisted.

Cover letters

You can't just submit a CV or an application; you also need to send a cover note. Follow a structured approach to dramatically increase your chances of getting shortlisted. See Chapter 11.

The hidden job market

People talk about the hidden job market as if it's a big secret, but it just means contacting organizations direct. You need to be bold and be ready for setbacks. As this is likely to be the best way to get a job offer, you'll be pleased that the process is explained simply in Chapter 12.

The interview

Woo hoo! All your work has been worth it and you've been shortlisted. We've got all about the interview covered in Chapters 13 and 14.

Phone and Skype interviews

There's a different approach needed when you are interviewed by phone or Skype, and you will find the essentials in Chapter 15.

Staying motivated

It's going to take time to get the job, so you need to keep yourself motivated. Chapter 16 has this covered.

The job offer

It's great news to get the job offer, but let's make sure you should say yes in Chapter 17.

2. Be clear on your goal

Before focusing on looking for a job, you need to be clear on what you want to do. Having a clear idea of the job you want means that every aspect of your job search is focused on achieving your objective.

Do you know what you want to do? You need to identify a career that will excite you but that is also one where you are likely to be successful, even if it may entail further training or experience, otherwise you are setting yourself up to fail.

The easiest job to get is one that is similar to the job you already have (or had), or the next level up, and in a similar company. It is more challenging – although not impossible – to make a change; it can involve a drop in salary and will definitely require you to be absolutely clear on **why** you want this change of career and **how** you match up.

You have focus when you know what you want to do. Your goal may be difficult to achieve right now, so break it down and think about what jobs could be a step on the way to where you want to be. This will help you choose a job wherein you will gain relevant experience that will enhance future applications.

Jenny knew she wanted a career in marketing, and also knew that competition was tough, so she works as a temp in a marketing agency, helping her to make contacts, find out more about the industry and enhance her CV for her next application.

Keith wanted to stay within the finance field after redundancy – and knows that his 15-year track record will appeal to other companies. Within just a few months he is successful in finding a new role.

Sue wanted to keep her options open and applied for everything she thought she could do, but her CV was vague, she couldn't be specific when telling others what she wanted and four months on is despondent – she can't understand why she has only been shortlisted once.

Many people seek to keep their options open but as Sue (in the above case study) found, this can make it harder to create a clear message, whether you are talking to somebody or revising your CV. It also means you are going to find it hard to do sufficient research – you can't look in depth if you are focused on too many options.

The choice you make is not for ever – indeed a career for life is now a rarity. You are making the choice for your next job. Some people will work towards a defined career path. For others it will be a job for the next couple of years, where they gain experience and then reconsider the direction they will go in.

Most people make a career decision based on their career history. They look at their CV and choose a job to apply for based on what they have done before. This can often be the easiest way to get a new job, and if you need to get a job quickly, this may be your best option. Once settled in a new job, you can then take time to explore what you would really want to do and plan a move to achieve your new goal.

It's always worth spending time reviewing who you are and making a decision on what it is that you want to do. The rest of this chapter takes you through practical exercises to aid your career decision-making.

Let's start by looking back to when you were younger.

Looking back to childhood

What did you love to do when you were young? What subjects did you enjoy at school? How did you spend your spare time? What activities made you lose track of time? Make a note. Often these activities had real meaning for us and they may provide inspiration for a career change or ideas for how to tweak a job.

 James, who loved to draw, became an accountant because his parents said it would be a secure job. Carrie, who loved to mend and make things,

9

didn't pursue a career path like engineering but instead moved into retail management, as she wanted to fit in with her friends. Both may be good at the jobs they have chosen but believe there is a more fulfilling career for them elsewhere.

Who are you?

Alongside looking back into childhood, we can also think about the type of person we are – quiet, thoughtful people are drawn to different jobs than outgoing people. Make a note of the many ways in which you can describe yourself; start by looking at the list opposite for ideas. You may like to add to this over the next few days.

Skills – what can you do?

Skills are the things we have learned to do, gained through both work experience and hobbies. They fall into a number of categories such as communication skills, interpersonal skills, leadership skills, organizational skills, analytical skills, problem-solving skills, financial skills, numerical skills, practical skills and creative skills.

Make a note of your top skills – what are the tasks that you are praised for achieving, and what are you qualified to do? It's not just about what you have done in your current or most recent job; skills can include things you do outside of your main, paid work such as a hobby or interest. As you write down your top skills, there will be some that you don't

Achievement-driven
Adaptable
Adventurous
Aggressive
Analytical
Assertive
Astute
Bashful
Careful
Caring
Competitive
Confident
Creative
Curious
Decisive
Dependable
Disciplined
Dominant
Efficient
Empathic
Expedient
Focused
Forgiving
Imaginative
Impulsive
Introspective
Logical
Methodical

Modest
Objective
Patient
Persistent
Practical
Precise
Punctual
Realistic
Reserved
Resilient
Resourceful
Self-critical
Sensitive
Sociable
Straightforward
Strategic thinker
Tactful
Talkative
Task-orientated
Tense
Tolerant
Traditional
Unassuming
Understanding
Versatile
Weak
Worrier

enjoy using, so cross these out. With the ones that remain, make sure you are specific. For example, which are better: your written or verbal communication skills? Are your verbal skills better in one-to-one situations or in large groups? Providing an example of using each skill will be very useful for revising your CV and to discuss at interview.

Interests

Make a note of everything you enjoy doing. This does not need to be focused purely on work tasks; thinking more broadly can generate possibilities. Even if you can't directly use your interest in a specific job, it can help with the work setting. For example, if you are an accountant with a love of art, you could seek opportunities within art galleries, museums etc.

Lucy completed this exercise and realized that she had always thought of herself as creative, witty and outgoing, so why was she working as a contracts manager in an organization where these characteristics were not highly valued? She was good at her job – she could pay attention to detail and was able to communicate effectively both in writing and in person. She loved music – she went to gigs and kept in touch with new music through internet radio shows. The exercise resulted in her considering a career reviewing contracts within the music business.

Nick was an unhappy lawyer who loved golf. He wondered if it would be possible to follow his dream of becoming a golf pro. It was, and he is!

Personality and environment

John Holland, a US psychologist, developed a theory that vocational interests are a result of personality, so people will express their personality through their career choices as well as through their hobbies. His theory divides people and jobs into six broad areas: Realistic, Investigative, Artistic, Social, Enterprising and Conventional. Read the descriptions of these six different groups below and choose the two that most resonate with you.

Realistic: Jobs which fall into this category involve operating machinery, providing security, using computers or outdoor jobs including farming. Hobbies probably include being outdoors – hiking, camping, being active, building or repairing things. You are probably noted for mechanical ingenuity and dexterity, physical coordination and common sense.

Investigative: Jobs which fall into this category involve research, science, mathematics and working in a lab, doing research and solving abstract problems. Hobbies may include reading, playing strategy games and doing puzzles. You are probably noted for being intellectually curious and analytical.

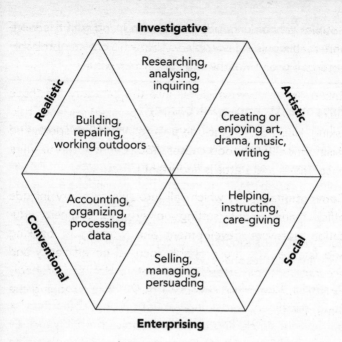

Investigative

Researching, analysing, inquiring

Realistic

Building, repairing, working outdoors

Artistic

Creating or enjoying art, drama, music, writing

Conventional

Accounting, organizing, processing data

Helping, instructing, care-giving

Social

Selling, managing, persuading

Enterprising

Artistic: Jobs which fall into this category include creating art, writing, performing, and composing music. Hobbies may include listening to music, visiting art galleries and museums, going to the theatre, producing art and playing music. You are probably noted for being imaginative, independent and creative.

Social: Jobs which fall into this category are those which demonstrate listening skills, verbal ability and people skills, including teaching, counselling, healthcare and religion.

Hobbies probably include volunteering, community service and reading self-development books. You are probably noted for your empathy and concern for others.

Enterprising: Jobs which fall into this category are those which involve selling, managing, persuading and risk-taking. Hobbies may include politics, adventure sports and raising money for good causes. You probably like to influence others and status is important to you.

Conventional: Jobs which fall into this category include office management, setting up systems, business education, software development and working in banking and finance. You are probably focused on efficiency and accuracy and pay attention to detail. Hobbies probably include volunteering, collecting things and managing the family finances.

Look at the two which appeal to you the most and you might find yourself pulled in different ways. For example, you may be seen by everyone as a brilliant computer programmer, but this is ignoring the side of you that enjoys spending time with people. Perhaps you were able to combine the two while at university but your computer-programming job involves too much time spent alone.

This can help you make sense of why you are unhappy or dissatisfied, and help you decide what you want to do.

It's not just about the job – your working environment

You should also consider the type of working environment that suits you. If you are someone with strong artistic tendencies, you will probably prefer a more creative environment rather than a conventional one such as working in a bank or insurance company. If you are someone who prefers conventional interests you are unlikely to be happy in a creative environment and would prefer a more office-based one.

Do you have any preferences for things such as job structure, career path, working hours, commuting distance, office location and environment, minimum salary and ideal benefits? The clearer you are, the easier it will be to focus. What sort of environment would enable you to work at your best? Consider the type of organization, culture, salary, location and anything else you can think of.

Consider the size of organization. For example, you could be a catering supervisor in a large organization and move to be a catering manager in a smaller organization. Or be a general manager in a smaller company and change to an operations manager in a medium-sized company.

If your maximum commuting time is 30 minutes, it may seriously constrain your search, so could you extend it to 60 minutes? But be realistic – there's no point getting excited if you see an ideal job and then realize it's 100 miles from your home.

CASE STUDY

Cheryl was made redundant from her highly paid job as a financial analyst. Her ideal working day would be up to a 30-minute journey from home and with the freedom to work from home at least one day a week. She was willing to earn less if it meant she could work with a company she believed in. Employment as a finance manager in the charity sector would match many of her needs.

It is important to be clear on what you want to do. Knowing yourself, knowing more about the job you seek, and being clear about how you match up will dramatically increase your chance of success. Fail to do this and you will be one of the many who browse through job sites in the hope that something appeals. This means you will never be fully focused on a job and success in an application is less likely.

Knowing who you are and what you want to do means that your CV, cover letter, LinkedIn profile and so on are consistent. It also makes it much easier when you meet with people; you are clear on what you want to do and can clearly state what you seek. This applies when meeting people both in person and via platforms such as LinkedIn.

Making your choice

You can't get a job till you know what you want. It's not down to a recruitment agency or HR department to work out what it is you should be doing. Everything you include in your CV and letter must be focused on the job you want.

You can do much more self-analysis, and many do, but if you need a job quickly, it's better to make a decision now so you can focus on your job search. Are you happy that you have now identified a suitable job, and the ideal location and environment? If not, what more do you need to find out?

It may be a specific job, or it may be a broader area. The clearer you are on the sort of job you want, the easier it will be when other people ask you what you are looking for. So write it down. Does this answer the question of the type of job you are seeking, the sort of company, etc.? Read it out loud and fine-tune it till it sounds natural. (You will find more detail on how to be clear on what you want in Chapter 8, 'Creating your message – the pitch'.)

But it's not just about what *you* want – you must also make sure you focus on the needs of the organization. Doing research (see the next chapter for more on this) will ensure you focus your message on what the company wants.

Finally, while you have identified a job to apply for, you must check that jobs in this area are going to be advertised. Ideally you will be looking for a job in a growing market.

When you still don't know

Many people need more extensive help in making a career choice, such as that provided by a registered guidance practitioner, chartered psychologist or career coach. You can get an idea of the help on offer by looking at the websites of reputable career-coaching companies. My own company, Amazing People, provides a good benchmark in the UK.

For many, the use of assessments can be highly valuable. There are several well-known career assessments, with the Highlands Ability Battery, Myers Briggs Type Indicator, Strong Interest Inventory and Talent Q Dimensions among the most useful. Again, seek the advice of a reputable career-coaching company if you think you would benefit from an assessment.

Setting goals

Now you are clear on what you want, you need to make sure you communicate this clearly – don't be vague, have a focused outcome. Then, when you have a meeting, you will be clear on what you want: a follow-up appointment, an introduction, etc. Having an end in mind makes it much easier to focus; otherwise, it is like setting out on a journey with no clear idea of where you are going.

Most of us know about SMART goals, but then forget to think about each element. For your job search plan you need to be setting SMARTER goals:

- You need a goal which is SPECIFIC. You are sure what you want to achieve. What job are you looking for?

- It needs to be MEASURABLE; you need to know where you start from so you can monitor progress. Getting the new job is a clear measure of success but also break it down into sub-steps such as: revise CV, research the current challenges in the industry, etc.

- The goal has to be ACHIEVABLE. Perhaps you need to take smaller steps: firstly to get a job as a marketing assistant, then marketing executive as you work towards being a marketing director.

- It also has to be REALISTIC – if we find science confusing, will we ever pass the exams to qualify as a nutritionist? Are there better alternatives?

- TIME BOUND means we have a timescale to achieve. Talk to people and get a sense of how long it will take to move from x to y. Work out all the sub-steps and create a timeline.

- The goal should also be EXCITING; it should have personal meaning. It has to be something you want to do. Make sure it makes you want to get on and get there.

- Finally, it should be RECORDED. Write it down and monitor progress; get your goal, and all the sub-goals, written down and in your diary, on your phone, on the wall …

This chapter has helped you to clarify what it is you want to do; you can now focus on your research.

3. Understand your target using research

Effective job hunting involves effective research, finding out as much as possible about jobs, your preferred career path, and the organization you will apply to. You can then make focused applications. But that's not the end – you will need to do further research to enhance an application and again before the interview. You will want to return to this chapter at various times on your job search journey.

When you research, you start broad as you decide on the type of work you want to do and then focus in greater detail. The following image makes this clear.

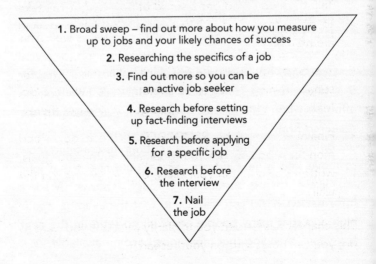

1. Broad sweep – find out more about how you measure up to jobs and your likely chances of success

2. Researching the specifics of a job

3. Find out more so you can be an active job seeker

4. Research before setting up fact-finding interviews

5. Research before applying for a specific job

6. Research before the interview

7. Nail the job

1. Broad sweep

You won't want to go after a job that you have no likelihood of getting, so see how you measure up. Each country will have relevant websites to use, such as in the UK the **National Careers Service** or in the USA O*net online. Using sites like these will help you to see if you have a background that will make it reasonably easy to make the move, or indicate the development you will need to be a credible candidate.

This research is powerful; it will stop you heading for disappointment. Far better to realize now that you need more experience as a training officer before you are a credible candidate as a training manager, or that you need more experience and a qualification before you are ready to apply to be a marketing manager, so a job as a marketing assistant might be the better one to apply for.

Don't stick at your desk, talk with people as well. This may help you identify alternative routes to a job, or reveal that you may not need a particular qualification. Chapter 5 is dedicated to fact-finding interviews to help you be effective when talking with people, but you **must do the research first.**

Before you spend too much time researching how to move into a new industry, you should check that jobs are likely to be available. Through **Labour Market Information (LMI)** you might find that the average age is high and that many people are likely to retire in the next few years, meaning that more jobs become available, or it may predict whether a particular job is likely to be moved overseas.

LMI provides detail on what is happening in the world of work, so you can make realistic plans for your future. It covers topics such as the number and type of job vacancies, trends in different parts of the country and what employers are looking for, so is an essential part of your job search.

2. Researching the specifics of a job

As you identify a job to apply for, start to look at the job ads and identify the most commonly mentioned characteristics. You can then ensure that these key words and qualities are used in both your CV and any communication (letter or email) you send to people within an organization.

3. Find out more so you can be an active job seeker

Once you are clear about the job and type of industry you are targeting, you can get ready to be active. Activity will cover both research to identify further information and then jobs to apply for and further details are in this chapter.

An internet search will identify relevant recruitment consultants to approach. You can check through ads to identify relevant companies, and also search via LinkedIn and through talking with others.

Find out about a company that may be expanding through the business press; there may be short posts on who is moving into new premises and so on. You may read that an organization has gained a new contract which could mean that additional jobs may become available. Don't just look for jobs you could do, see if higher-level posts are being advertised; jobs lower down in the organization might become available later.

Research an industry using a business library who should provide resources for you to identify lists of privately owned companies. From these you can access company information – not only addresses, but also performance and structure, product information, who makes what and where it can be bought, and market research information.

You can also request copies of annual reports through the company's PR department.

4. Research before setting up fact-finding interviews

Research has to be undertaken before a fact-finding interview (about which you will read more in Chapter 5). It is highly frustrating to someone who has given up 30 minutes of their time when they have someone asking questions to which they could easily have found the answers online. Finding out as much as possible will help you to identify the right questions to ask.

 You must do as much research as you can before a fact-finding interview, otherwise it's a wasted opportunity.

5. Research before applying for a specific job

Once you have done your research and identified the role you seek, you can conduct further research in order to revise your CV and create a targeted cover letter. Look at job ads to identify the key words used for a particular job. A great approach is to gather 4–6 different ads and notice the words that are common across all ads for a similar role. You can then ensure that these key words are included in your CV, online applications and so on.

Through forums you could chat and get details on other people's experiences with an organization for which you have been shortlisted. A Google search will find relevant forums, and don't forget to look for relevant groups on LinkedIn.

Your research can include checking if the company has a good reputation and is financially sound. This could be vital if you are giving up a secure job and want to know if the new organization is likely to be safe. It will also help you to understand both the organization and the industry so you can ask intelligent questions at interview.

Far too many people think a quick look at an organization's website counts as research. This is the bare minimum; you need to do much more, including finding forums to access customer comments. You should know the answers to the following:

- What exactly does this organization do? You may want to be a finance officer but you should still find out about the product or services. An interviewer is likely to ask you what you know. Wow them with your knowledge.

- The financial status of the company – how do this year's results compare with those of the last three years? What question could you ask at interview to demonstrate you took the time to find this out?

- What do people think? Look on forums to find out customer comments.

- Based on your research, what do you see as the key successes of the past year and the challenges for the forthcoming year?

- How does this organization compare to its competitors?

- What's happening in the news, both for this organization and for the industry? Where are the opportunities, what impact will government initiatives have?

As you apply, you can search for news about the organization so you can start your letter by referring to what you have read, such as a problem, and your possible solution.

6. Research before the interview
When you get shortlisted for interview, you can search for the interviewer on the Internet to see if there are any mentions, or articles, in the press, and details of conferences attended, etc. Such information is very useful as you can

use it to help create a question to ask, or find a way to refer to it in your introduction.

Alongside researching the company you have got an interview with, also look at the websites of competitors to understand the differences and enable you to have a view on the organizational challenges your potential new employer will face.

 Set up Google alerts so you receive daily updates on anything related to the job you want.

 Identify relevant professional associations. For example, if you want to move into Purchasing you can join the relevant professional association – in the UK this would be the Chartered Institute of Purchasing and Supply (CIPS) – receive their journal and attend local meetings, thus developing contacts.

The question 'What do you know about us?' is very common. Employers want applicants who have had the initiative and enthusiasm to find out something about the organization. Stand out by showing you have gone beyond a review of their website. You will have already done this to target your application; you can now do a final review and see if there is anything relevant in the news so you can demon-strate your knowledge of the company and industry.

Next time you go for an interview armed with all rel-evant information, knowing who you are seeing, what the company does and who its competitors are, you will feel more confident and have a better sense of what you are letting yourself in for.

Enough research, time to get talking with people. The next two chapters will guide you.

4. Networking

'Everything that happens in your career always starts with someone you know. You don't need to surf the net. Your next big break will not come from some mysterious technology or discovery of new information. Your next break will come from someone you know.'
—Derek Sivers, founder and former president of CD Baby

So many people hate the thought of networking, and avoid it. Sometimes we need to challenge our fears, especially if, as in the case of networking, they involve an important part of our job search strategy. I don't want to make you uncomfortable, but I do believe it is helpful to step a little way outside your comfort zone. It can help to reframe the situation – you are not trying to sell yourself but seeking to connect with others.

Networking is not about hassling people but about letting other people know what you are looking for. Often it's about reconnecting with people you already know, or being put in touch with someone through a mutual acquaintance. It is very important to make it quite clear that what you are seeking is advice and ideas, and that you are not asking for a job.

In Mark Granovetter's study *Getting a Job: A Study of Contacts and Careers* (University of Chicago Press, 1995), 56 per cent of people found jobs through personal contacts. Most of these jobs were found through weak ties: loose acquaintances rather than the strong ties of close friends.

The people we see on a regular basis are people with whom we share a lot in common – we have similar interests, and enjoy similar activities. When looking for new ideas it can be more helpful to get in touch with people with whom we have a more casual relationship. Through them we can be introduced to new people and they can take a different view on our situation.

Thinking of who to contact, we can choose family and close friends, people we have worked with, but also the weaker ties of people we know from school and university and those we have met through our local church, the tennis club, our neighbours and so on. Each of these people also has a network of people they know.

We can expand our network of people by talking to people outside our normal circle of friends, or through voluntary work. We can also get involved with a professional body, so for example if you are seeking a job in HR, join and attend local meetings of the Chartered Institute of Personnel and Development (CIPD).

Start by making a list of everyone you know. You could use categories such as family, friends, current work colleagues, clients and suppliers, previous bosses and colleagues, neighbours, people you know through clubs and organizations, friends from university and school, friends of your children or parents.

Now review your list. You can't contact everyone on it, so **prioritize your top ones**.

Your top contacts are anyone who:

- Is knowledgeable about the industries in which you are interested and may have key contacts who can help you with advice or information (it can be really helpful to connect with someone at the same organizational level as you but who works in a different function, so they can refer you to a peer)

- Can tell you about real opportunities and refer you to someone who can arrange a meeting and read your CV

- May be unlikely to have immediate contacts, but may be a source of useful ideas.

Alongside talking with people you know, you can specifically seek out people who may be able to help you get the job you want. You can find people to contact through a number of methods, including:

- Attending professional meetings and conferences

- Working as a volunteer or serving on a committee

- Contacting alumni of your university.

Networking is not only done face to face – online can be very powerful. In particular, participating in discussions on LinkedIn can be very helpful (see Chapter 9).

Keeping track

It's all too easy to lose track of the people you are in touch with, so use Excel or similar to set up a spreadsheet of the following:

- Name and title of person
- Name of assistant who answers the phone and any other useful numbers
- Who referred you
- Date of each phone call and/or meeting
- Topics discussed
- Personal insights
- Referrals, if any
- Follow up action required.

You are now ready to network.

Being specific about the help you want – the type of job, and type of organization that interests you – will make it easier for the other person to think of possible jobs. When you get in touch, remind people of your background and experience – even our friends may be unsure of the detail of our jobs.

The meeting – first contact

You can now choose the first ten people to get in touch with. Decide whether your initial contact will be by phone, email or letter. A phone call will work well with someone you know but with busy people, you may not be able to get through. Email is easy, but can easily be deleted; a letter is more likely to be opened. Always include a link to (or at least give the address of) your LinkedIn page. I suggest sending out a short letter, and following up with a phone call. That way, the person will be expecting your call and may have left a message with their assistant if unavailable.

When you phone or write, include a short review of what you have been doing. Say that you are seeking advice and suggestions to help with your job search. (Chapter 5, on fact-finding interviews, will provide details of how to do this.)

 With emails, create a signature line so that all job emails can go out with your contact details automatically included at the end of each mailing.

If you choose to write, the letter overleaf should provide a good start, ready for you to adapt to your situation.

When you phone, the other person will probably think you are looking for a job, so you need to emphasize that you are in a research phase and are checking to be sure that your skills will be needed in, for example, the charity sector. You then ask for the meeting. A phone call could go something like this:

Dear Charles,

I am taking the opportunity to write to you, as I would welcome some input regarding the next phase of my career.

Having developed my skills and experience as a marketing executive in the telecommunications industry, I am considering transferring my skills to the not-for-profit sector.

You know a lot about the charity sector and I should be glad of your advice and to hear about current conditions. I have enclosed my CV to bring you up to date with what I have been doing over the last few years and would appreciate meeting up with you soon.

I will phone you next week to find out when you are free.

Yours sincerely,

Kris Jameson

'Hello, agreed Simon Jones suggested I call you – do you know Simon?'

'Yes I do.'

'Simon said that you would be a good person to talk with to help with my job search research. Did you get my letter?'

'Yes, I did.'

'Is now a good time to talk?'

'Yes it's fine.'

'I'm doing research into [name the organization's business, e.g. charity marketing] and my research suggested your organization has a strong reputation [or is a market leader]. Could you spare 20 minutes at the end of the day to answer some questions?'

'What specifically would you like to find out?'

'The challenges facing the sector and the types of charity that are likely to appreciate someone with my background in the telecommunications industry. An introduction to some charities would be brilliant. I've identified about six charities I'd like to approach, plus I have a list of questions.'

'Why not email me your list so I can see who I know there and I'll answer your questions by email.'

'Thank you, I'll get the list emailed over later today and could we then meet up in a couple of weeks?'

'Yes, that's fine.'

Then set up a meeting.

We can feel a little embarrassed at asking for help, but if someone were to phone you requesting ideas and advice, you are likely to want to help. Other people will want to help you too! Start with the people you know.

Schedule a face-to-face meeting

Make an appointment and perhaps meet them for a coffee close to their place of work. Some people can be hard to contact, but do persevere; relationships build much quicker when you can meet face to face. The second choice is to meet via Skype so you still have a visual connection.

Do keep to the time scheduled – a maximum of 20–30 minutes – and make it clear that you don't expect a job offer. Make it clear you seek advice.

In the meeting you can summarize your own background, show them your CV and ask if you should make any changes. Outline your job search strategy, ask for comments on its viability within the sector and listen to their answer. They may be prepared to evaluate a target list of companies if you have one, or may know some senior people to whom they can provide an introduction.

As you talk you may like to find out:

- General advice about business opportunities

- Information about any possible leads or information in the area, or industries in which you are interested. Your contact may know, for instance, that a company is expanding or moving into the area, etc.

- Information about specific requirements

- Names, addresses and phone numbers of any contacts who can give further help along the lines of the above, and the best means for contacting them.

You could also ask someone who knows you well if you could include them as a referee or if they would write you an open letter of recommendation, or a recommendation on LinkedIn.

Effective communication

Listening shows your interest. You will learn useful facts about the present state of the industry and should be ready to move away from your prepared list of questions. If appropriate, you could ask if any consultancy work is needed. Whether paid or initially unpaid, this might lead to a permanent job, full- or part-time. At the end, ask for referrals. These could be for future fact-finding interviews or job leads.

People are more likely to help when we have rapport. You can demonstrate this through mirroring posture and voice tone. If you are in rapport you will probably find yourself leaning forward as they do, or notice that you both have your left hand cupping your chin. You mustn't be seen to be mimicking but as you concentrate on developing a good relationship with someone, you may do this naturally.

People's voice tone can be high or low, loud or soft; it really helps if you speak with a similar tone. If you have a very deep voice and you are speaking to someone with a much higher-pitched voice, you may want to make subtle adjustments to your voice tone.

Think about your body language and facial expression, your posture and gestures; again, they should be similar to those of the person you are talking with. And don't forget eye contact – you must look at the other person.

You can adjust your language depending on how someone best perceives a situation. Some of us are visual: we remember images; other people are tonal and remember words; still others are kinaesthetic and remember a feeling.

You can find out which mode someone is most likely to use by asking a question and noticing which way they look. If they look up, they are remembering a picture: visual. If they look to the side, they are auditory, and if they are looking down, they are remembering a feeling. You can enhance your rapport with someone by using the right language to reinforce what you say.

Visual: 'I see what you mean', 'I get the picture', 'My perspective on this'

Auditory: 'That rings a bell', 'I hear you', 'That sounds like'

Kinaesthetic: 'Can't get a grip on', 'I feel', 'It boils down to'

Follow up

Always thank the person for their help. We all want to help others, and when we do, we want to know that we made a difference. It could be a phone call, an email, a postcard – anything that says 'thank you for going out of your way to help me'. So send a timely thank you note. Don't miss this opportunity to be in front of your contacts again.

Keep your contacts informed of your progress with the companies and people to whom you have been introduced. This will maintain their interest and keep you in their mind, so that they will continue to pass on useful names and/or information. As your networking progresses, you are moving into active job search (more on this in Chapter 12).

CASE STUDY

I recently worked with Henry. He has identified what he wants to do: to use his acting skills within a murder mystery company. He has found out details on different companies, identified their requirements (complete a form; send a CV by post, not email, etc.) and will follow up accordingly. He was then unsure what else to do. So we talked about where he can meet people who work in this area – through online forums and by arranging in-person meetings.

It's unlikely that the people he meets are directly working in this area – it would be a bonus if they did – but they might know someone who does.

Henry won't start by asking them this directly, but will show interest and get to know them. He will then ask the question. Probably the person doesn't know anyone, but he won't stop there!

He should have some business cards ready to hand out. These can be done very cheaply but some of the low-cost suppliers will print their own marketing details on the reverse, so you may want to opt for professionally printed cards. Henry can then end the conversation by asking them to get in touch if they think of anyone he could contact and handing over his card, getting their card or contact details in exchange. He can then follow up a few days later with something relevant to their needs, perhaps an article.

A networking plan

If you are unemployed you should be spending at least three to four hours a day in active job searching, and most of this should be meeting people or being active through online discussions. If, for example, you have seen a job advertised as a buyer with the ABC Company, seek to find someone who can give you the inside story on what is happening in the company – information that is only available to employees. You can also search on LinkedIn (see Chapter 9).

You can also find out the name of the HR manager and the head buyer, then Google their names to identify their interests and activities, so if the head buyer is going to be at an event, you can attend and thus bump into them in a less formal setting.

Sometimes we may not be sure what to say to new people. At a more formal networking event you could ask questions such as:

- I've only just joined, is there a good way to get more involved?

- Have you come across the speaker's work before?

- He brought a book out last year, have you read it?

- This session is about social media, have you found it helpful with your career?

- What do you know about this topic?

- What do you do?

- What's the biggest challenge that your organization is facing at the moment?

They will then ask you questions, so be ready with your pitch. Let them know the type of person or organization you want to meet and then follow up later to keep your 'name in the frame'.

 Social psychologists study **impression manage-ment**, a theory which states that the impressions people gain of us are congruent with the impression we want to convey. We can use this in our search for a new job. If we want to move into a new work area, we can increase our chances of success by demonstrating that we share the same values as the people currently working in that area. If you find that the managers working at the company you want to join all belong to a particular organization such as the Rotary Club, you could choose to join so as to meet them on a social basis. In discussion you could demonstrate similar views rather than challenge the group view on social topics such as government initiatives.

Other ways to network (networking for introverts)
Networking is quite a sociable activity; you are getting out there and meeting people. Not everyone finds this easy,

and we may not want to put ourselves in this situation too often.

If you are more introverted by nature, not someone who gains their energy from being with other people, and find being with many new people a stressful experience, you may prefer to choose online networking through discussion forums and LinkedIn and getting yourself known through a personal blog or by writing an article.

There are many discussion groups out there but I would recommend starting with LinkedIn. With 500,000 groups, there must be many that are relevant to you. You can also find groups through Google and Yahoo. The groups you may like to join will vary immensely, so use a search facility for e.g. forums and marketing. When I did this, one of the links was to http://www.marketingmixers.com. The site says:

On these sites, you won't want to go straight in and ask for a job. It's more about increasing the people you know and being helpful. You need to get a feel for these sites before you comment (known as 'lurking'), but do look for where you can add helpful comments, thus enhancing your reputation. Many sites will allow you to add a signature line where you can add some personal details of yourself, with your contact details clearly stated.

5. Fact-finding interviews

I think fact-finding (or informational) interviews are truly brilliant. They help you to find out more about an organization or role, and as you aren't directly asking for a job, you are far more likely to get a positive response. You choose this approach when you are uncertain whether to apply for a particular role and seek further information to enable you to enhance any future application.

You use networking skills, as covered in the previous chapter, but now you go much deeper to find out more about a job or company. The networking chapter reminds you of the need to build effective connections with others and not to go directly in with what you want.

You then move onto fact-finding interviews to seek out information.

People like to help other people, and a clear request for help through a meeting results in success around 50 per cent of the time (before the recession of the late 2000s and early 2010s, a 90 per cent success rate was common, but now more people are following this approach and people are busy …). However, many people do this badly: they are demanding, don't personalize, and expect the reader to follow up. You will do much better if you follow the advice in this chapter.

You need to be clear why you are getting in touch: you are not asking for a job but seeking to find out more information. And you must follow up – you can't expect them to get back to you. It's your priority, not theirs.

There are three reasons to use this type of interview:

1. When you have already done a lot of research and now need to talk to someone who has practical experience of a particular job so you can see how well it measures up to your expectations

2. When you know what you want to do and are looking for a way to enhance your likelihood of success in getting a job

3. When you really want a job in a particular company or industry, and you are gathering further intelligence to enhance an application or to make a direct approach.

Fact-finding interviews help you begin to build a relationship with someone who works for the organization you want to work for, and this can help later when you apply for a job or take the direct approach. In very competitive fields this will really enhance any application you make. You will learn more about the field and the organization from someone currently working in that area and can use this to tailor your application.

A successful fact-finding interview can lead on to a request to shadow somebody for a day or more. You will learn far more, for example, about being an investment banker by shadowing one for a day, than through taking on a back-office admin job for three months.

You can arrange fact-finding interviews by a referral or a 'cold call'.

 You must have undertaken online research before making contact. It's extremely irritating to be asked questions which could have been answered via the Internet.

The same principles outlined in the previous chapter in relation to networking apply to arranging fact-finding interviews. So send a short email (or go retro and send a letter!), and follow up with a phone call.

When you get in touch, clearly state your purpose. Be brief and concise. Ensure you come across as someone they will want to meet. Demonstrate that you have already done some research. Include some highlights from your CV. If you have found them via a referral, say so. If not, look for common interests; offer congratulations on an accomplishment or show curiosity about the organization or industry.

If you make your approach personal, so it does not look like something you are sending out to lots of people, you are more likely to get people to say yes. If your approach isn't working, you need to check that you aren't being too pushy. Think from the other person's perspective and write something memorable that will grab their attention.

Follow up with a call to set up the appointment. Some people suggest calling after 5.30pm when an assistant might have left for the day. You should ideally try to talk with at least three people who are actually doing the job that interests you, so be prepared to get in touch with five or six people.

Here's a real letter from a client that got a meeting.

Dear Geoff

I noticed your profile on LinkedIn and thought it might be an idea to send you a note.

I have recently spoken with Eric van Olsen (who sends his regards) and he recommended I should get in contact.

My expertise is supply chain management and I am now very interested in a move into project management consultancy. My research has identified Jones & Jones as leaders in this field.

My career to date has covered most aspects of customer service and supply chain management. In the recent past I was project manager for a warehouse centralization project within Schmidt GmbH.

Prior to that I was a member of the procurement team involved in a pan-European roll-out of the XYZ ERP system. During the XYZ project I spent extended periods in Shanghai and Munich working with Schmidt colleagues and also the consultants (Omega Lambda). At the end of the project the teams dispersed to their home countries to successfully implement XYZ. This was carried out together with the consultants from Omega Lambda.

Would you be able to give me 20–30 minutes of your day to gather further information and advice on pursuing career possibilities in consultancy? Alternatively if you feel a colleague might be more appropriate, perhaps you could let me know.

I will phone your office next Wednesday 25th April to discuss a convenient time to meet.

Thank you in advance for your help and I would be happy to send my CV to yourself or your contacts in the interim.

Yours sincerely,

David Pearson

Here's the introduction to Fiona's letter which demonstrates a different way of opening a letter.

I am very interested in moving into a service management role within the Financial Services industry. I'm currently researching to ensure this is the right move to make, and as you are highly experienced in this area, I would love to speak with you in order to gain a better understanding of the work involved and how well my current skill set may transfer.

And Paul concluded with an alternative way to end a letter:

I understand you are giving a seminar at City College next week and I was wondering if you were free to meet for a coffee afterwards? I am at the moment looking for advice on the best way to approach working as a consultant to a voluntary sector such as yours, as you have a career path similar to mine.

I will phone your office next Tuesday 24th April to discuss meeting up.

Prepare your questions

Before the time comes to make your follow-up phone call, you should have your questions prepared in case the person wants to go through them over the phone, there and then. That is not ideal – it is better to meet up – but sometimes people will want you to go ahead, so be ready.

Develop a list of questions; probably six to eight is the maximum you will get covered. You will identify some through your research but the following examples will also be helpful. Your first fact-finding interview will be broad and general but you will get more specific as you find out more.

You must undertake comprehensive research in advance, so your questions will focus on what you can't find online rather than waste an opportunity with basic-level questions.

You can ask questions which focus on the job, such as:

- What do you do during a typical working day or week?

- What do you find stressful, annoying and unpleasant about your work?

- What kind of challenges or problems do you have to deal with in this job?

- What do you find most satisfying and most frustrating about your job and field?

- How much do you work one to one with people?

- Do you find your work competitive or cooperative? Could you tell me more?

- How much deadline pressure comes with your job?

- What do you see as the future for this kind of work?

You can ask questions about their career choice:

- How did you decide to be a ...?

- What preparation, training, and/or experience did you have and what would you suggest for someone entering this field?

- Knowing what you know now, how would you have approached this career differently?

You can ask questions about their organization:

- What attributes, skills and backgrounds does your organization seek in new recruits?

- How do people find out about job openings in your organization? If through job sites, which ones? If word of mouth, who spreads the word?

You can ask questions about career planning:

- What advice do you have for someone interested in your work?

- If you were in my position, how would you go about getting into this field?

- What alternative options are there that don't need such a high level of qualification?

- What would I need to do to become an attractive candidate for a job in this field?

And you can also ask:

- What is the average starting salary for a person entering this career?

- Who else would you recommend or suggest I talk to, to learn more about this career?

- Do you have any other advice for me?

- May I contact you if other questions arise?

Phone call

Follow up your letter with a phone call to make an appointment. Ask for 20–30 minutes of their time. Sometimes people think you are looking for a job. Reassure them that you are not, that your focus is research into this particular career.

 Making these calls can be a bit stressful, especially the first time, so breathe deeply and act positive and upbeat. If you stand up when you speak it keeps your energy up and you will come across as more confident.

After you have been connected with the appropriate person, your conversation might sound like this:

> This is [your name]. I've been researching careers and have a strong interest in [make a note of the type of role, industry or organisation]. You are known as an expert in this area, and I would really appreciate an opportunity to meet up and talk with you about it.

Your next objective is to make the appointment. You could say, 'I believe that 30 minutes will be fine, although I will appreciate whatever time you are able to spend with me.'

Finally, thank them and conclude with a confirmation of the appointment date and time. You can email a note of thanks and confirm the appointment in writing.

At the meeting

The aim of a fact-finding interview is to find out more about a potential career, or to learn more to increase your chance of success.

The interview will also allow you to

- Show them that you value their time by being prepared; have your questions ready

- Ask for feedback on your CV, qualifications and proposed direction

- Ask for contacts who could help with advice and suggestions (NOT to request jobs from) and ideally for them to introduce you to them

- Ask permission to use the interviewer's name as an introduction if you are to contact them yourself

- Ask if you can help them in any way

- Ask permission to keep the interviewer informed of the progress you make.

And

- Don't criticize former colleagues or bosses.

- Smile and maintain good eye contact.

- Be prepared for the remote possibility that a job opportunity may enter the discussion.

- Write a thank you letter after the meeting.

If you are really interested in the career you've just explored, you can arrange to talk to others who work in this area. After you've thanked the individual for their time and effort, you might say:

I've learned a great deal today. Having heard about your organization, I'm interested in talking to more people about this field. I'm especially interested in [any special area that came up during your meeting]. Who do you think I should talk with next?

Be sure to phrase it that way. This is positive and assumes that they know someone (as opposed to 'Can you think of anyone I should talk with next?').

You may realize that this is not going to be the right career path to pursue, but you can still use this contact. You could say:

I really appreciate all of your time and effort today. Now that I've learnt more, I feel that I might be more effective in a smaller organization where I will not be called upon to specialize quite so much – at least, I need to find out. Who do you think I should talk with next?

Review

Reflection can be helpful. Review both the information you gained, and also how you came across. How can you improve for next time?

You may realize that you don't want to pursue this particular career path. Far better to find out now than three months into a new job! You can still use the referral approach. People belong to clubs or other organizations, and they may still know someone who can help you. Just tell the person what you're looking for on the basis of what you've learned. The referrals can be to similar fields or to totally different fields.

As your research progresses, your questions will become much more specific, something like: 'What kinds of opening in the advertising field are available for someone who loves to draw?' or 'I'm interested in computers, classical music and travel. Is there anything that could combine these interests?'

Whether you have confirmed that a job area is a good match for you, or have found out that a job isn't the one for you, both are valuable. Seek specific answers from as many people as you can, and don't forget to use LinkedIn.

6. The CV

It is *much* easier to create your CV once you know what it is that you want to do, otherwise you are likely to want to keep your options open, and your CV won't be focused on a particular job.

A bland, generic CV is unlikely to meet the requirements of any job.

As your CV will get less than a minute of someone's attention on a first sift, you need to grab the reader's attention, particularly when they look at the top half of your CV. This is what will appear on a computer screen before the person scrolls down. Your CV will first be looked at online, not printed, so make sure there is enough white space to make things stand out on a computer screen.

Your CV may not even be seen by a real person; most large employers use software to sift out who to shortlist. You need to make sure your CV includes specific key words and shows a good fit with the job description.

You probably already have a CV, so I want you to take a critical stance. Imagine you are shortlisting for the job you seek; would you shortlist you? We will review your CV section by section, but let's first take an overall view.

Given that only limited attention will be paid to your CV, you shouldn't try to include everything you can but focus your details on what is relevant to this particular job. The general view is that two sides of A4 is correct; with a limited work history it could be one-and-a-half sides, and a very senior executive may have three sides. Only provide a longer-length CV when it is absolutely essential.

You can help the recruiter by drawing their attention to key information through the use of **bold** and <u>underline</u>. You want to get your CV into the pile which has a second, more detailed review, and highlighting key information will help.

There are three types of CV:

- Chronological
- Skills-based
- Combination

So which should you choose?

The chronological CV – Choose this if you have a steady record of employment in an industry or functional area and want to stay in the same line of work. (If you are looking to change careers, or have been out of the job market for some time, you may prefer the skills-based CV.)

The skills-based CV – Too many potentially suitable applicants fail to get shortlisted due to the fact that they do not fit the expected applicant profile. A skills-based CV can help you to overcome this problem. With this type of CV, most of the first page lists relevant examples under the key requirements of the job, thus making it easy for someone to see how you will match up. Be aware though that some recruiters may wonder what you are trying to hide with this style of CV.

Let me now talk you through how to create a chronological CV. Even if you think a skills-based one will be best for you, it is still useful to create this style as well.

The chronological CV

Top of the CV

This is where you will include your name and contact details. You don't need to write 'Curriculum Vitae' in full at the top; people know what this document is. You also don't need all your contact details in large font. A great top to a CV is similar to this:

Sam Moore MBA http://www.linkedin.com/in/samkmoore	275 Wellington Road, Chester CH4 5TW 01244 123 456 07931 555 666 samkmoore@gmail.com

The name and contact details are clearly laid out and the link to the LinkedIn profile is available so the reader can quickly find out more about you. There is no need to include your national insurance number, marital status, driving licence details, etc. here; you would be wasting the most import-ant space on your CV. You may not need to include your postal address, given that nearly all correspondence is via email (and for personal security reasons) but make sure you have a personalized (and professional) voicemail message; you want anyone who calls you to be clear they have got through to the right person.

Profile and key words

Many people include a lengthy paragraph with an emphasis on what they want, but an organization is much less interested in what you want than in what you can do for it. So **make it succinct and pertinent to the job**. The organization doesn't care about you; it cares about its own situation. That's why research is important; it helps you understand the problems the organization faces so you can demonstrate how you can solve them.

When a CV is uploaded to a jobs database, companies will use applicant tracking software to search for relevant candidates using key words; so use relevant key words to increase the likelihood of being matched with a particular job. You can identify relevant key words to include through reviewing job ads for the job you seek.

Use enough key words to define your skills, experience, education, professional affiliations, etc. Increase your list of key words by including specifics; for example, list the names of software programs you use, but also include the key skills you possess that are needed for the job you are applying for. Include these key words throughout your CV as well.

One of my clients included a very short profile, but it made it very clear what she could offer the company, and this led to her being shortlisted:

Marketing Executive with five years' experience in FMCG, now ready to increase effectiveness for clients within a bespoke consultancy.

Others will include more detail such as:

Highly accomplished operations manager with a successful track record of consistently increasing revenue and slashing operating costs. Seeking a company who values high levels of customer focus accompanied by a desire to increase profitability in all areas of the business – money, staff morale, and environmental impact.

Employment history

When writing about their work history, lots of people make the mistake of listing their job description; they include lots of details on what they did rather than what they achieved. If you have done the same, you will need to rethink this section.

Here is a useful approach to take:

1. Write down details of each job you have had, including short-term assignments.

You are not necessarily going to include each one in your CV but you should be aware of the jobs you have had and the dates. There may be gaps between assignments, or when you went travelling or were job hunting; make sure that you have an accurate recall of where you worked, what you did and for how long.

Many people get confused as to who their employer is when they are a temporary worker. If you got the assignment via an agency, it is the agency that you worked for, not the company where you were assigned.

If you have had a number of short-term assignments you can group these together, such as:

Adecco, Employment Agency	**October 2010–April 2011**
A variety of short-term assignments working as an administrative assistant in the social care sector.	

You then include achievement bullets from different assignments underneath.

At all levels we can find ourselves working on short-term assignments. Jack worked for four companies in two years in his role as management accountant, due to taking on short-term contracts. He wanted to downplay this time as other jobs had lasted for three years or more, so on his CV he wrote:

62

1998–2000 Management Accountant
During this period, key positions were held with several large companies on fixed-term contracts including working with [company name] and [company name].

 If you have had a lot of jobs, including the dates on the right-hand side means they don't come across as important, as we read from left to right.

People are often unsure where to include voluntary work – within their work history or in a separate section. For most people, including it in their employment history will be the best place, but please make sure you indicate that it is voluntary and not salaried.

2. Identify and list achievement bullets

Now you have your list of jobs, you can start thinking about the tasks you did. Many people don't want to put in the effort to create achievement bullets, so instead they more or less copy and paste in details from their job description – but that approach won't get them shortlisted.

To create an effective CV you need to go beyond the list of tasks you did and focus on the impact on the company. I'm forever asking my clients, 'And what did that result in?'

You should aim to include three or four bullets under each job; perhaps up to six for your most recent job and fewer for earlier ones. Throughout, review what you have included and look for the link between this job and the job you are applying for.

Think about the different tasks you have done in your last job. Think of a problem you have had to solve or an opportunity you have taken advantage of. Which of your skills or strengths did you use, or what expertise? What was the benefit of this action? Is it possible to quantify what you did – did you save or make money or time, or reduce staffing costs? Start writing these down!

A couple of examples of achievement bullets should emphasize what's required.

- Worked with staff and associates to increase product turnover by 15 per cent and sales by 23 per cent.

- Trained fourteen new employees, five of whom were rapidly promoted. Devised and implemented a new sales training programme which resulted in a 37 per cent increase in new business.

Too often, people fail to emphasize their strengths. For example, writing 'Duties included supervision of staff' would have a much stronger impact if written as 'Successfully led a team of six, proving leadership and coaching which resulted in us being commended on our work by the MD'. Instead of 'Excellent communication skills', change to 'Complimented on my presentational skills, which included leading the winning pitch for a £50k project for my company'.

We create value in our job in different ways. We may not win a half-million-pound contract but we can be brilliant health and safety inspectors and save our company millions through ensuring people are safe and accidents do not occur. We could be brilliant waiters and so people come back to our restaurant time and time again and tell all their friends too. We could go that extra mile by providing a high level of customer care on the service desk at the garage, so customers come back each time their car needs a service and buy their next car from our company too. Think of examples similar to these to enhance this section of your CV.

Education, short courses and professional development

You will need to include details of your formal education. You don't have to include dates if you think it may lead to discrimination. As you get older, A-levels etc. are less likely to be relevant, but are worth including if you gained them as a mature student.

You should also include details of relevant short courses you have attended. Definitely include those which are relevant to the job you seek, but you can also include other courses that demonstrate your willingness to learn new things.

As preparation, make a note of each course you have been on, the date, how long it lasted and the benefits gained.

Include details of your computer literacy. List your level of competence in Word, Excel, etc. This is likely to be a self assessment if you are self-taught, unless you have gained a relevant qualification such as the European Computer Driving Licence.

How are your languages? This could help you to stand out. If you have a reasonable level of fluency it is worth mentioning it, but don't fib or you may find yourself being asked questions in the language you claim fluency in.

Professional memberships

If you have gained membership of organizations such as the Institute of Marketing, or are a Chartered Engineer, include details, with dates when membership was gained.

Personal interests/leisure activities

Should you include these? If you think they will give you an edge and you have an interesting story which links your interests to the job you seek then maybe it is worth it, but you can never be sure. We don't know the prejudices of the people who interview us – some people take an instant dislike to people who pursue a particular hobby. Include details of interests that are undertaken alone and you may not come across as a team player; too much on adventurous sports and the reader may wonder how much time you will take off sick with broken limbs. If you are going to include, for example, reading, make a note of the type of books you read and why. Rather than write 'Running', expand it to 'Training to complete a half-marathon in the spring'.

The skills-based CV

The preparation you have done for your chronological CV will also be useful for creating a skills-based CV but there will be a different focus. The main focus will be on how well you match up to the requirements of the job.

Lizzie wants to move into work as a legal executive. The key skills needed include:

- Excellent spoken and written communication skills
- The ability to explain legal matters clearly
- Patience, tact and discretion
- Good administrative and computer skills
- Accuracy and attention to detail
- Research skills
- An organized approach
- The ability to work under pressure.

She identified the requirements of this particular career through collecting ads for her chosen position and making a note of which key requirements appeared most frequently.

Lizzie uses the points above as the headings on side one of her CV. Under each, she gives examples of how her background meets that requirement.

This is then followed by a summary of her career history, which she keeps brief: just including job title, employer, and dates.

You will still include details of your education and training, as in a chronological CV.

Review

Your CV is not created in isolation but focused on the particular job you seek. Once you create your CV, give it an objective review. How well does it sell you for the job that you want? Ask people who work in HR or recruitment for advice, or people you talk with at fact-finding interviews: would they shortlist you?

If you cannot, you may need to think again about whether the job you have identified is a realistic aim at this stage of your career. Perhaps you need to gain extra experience, or make an interim job change before you are ready.

The text-based CV

Most internet job sites and online application forms will want you to paste your CV into boxes. Starting with a plain text version means you won't get unusual symbols as the job site software strips out your formatting.

To create a text-based CV, don't play about with your Word document; instead save your CV as a plain text file or copy it into a text editing program such as Notepad. Once you open it, you will see you have lost all formatting such as underlines, bold, fonts, etc.

You can improve the layout by using a hard return (use the 'Enter' button to start a new line). It might look OK in a word processing programme, but it can be very difficult to read via a text package without hard returns. You can make improvements to the style if you use CAPITAL LETTERS as headers.

Make sure you include **all** contact details on their own line, with a hard return in between.

Finalising your CV

Now you have completed your CV, leave it for at least 24 hours and then come back and review it. Ask yourself the following questions:

- Is it concise and clear? Make sure every word helps make the pitch. If your CV covers a page and a half, do not be tempted to fill the space.

- Does it grab attention? Highlight achievements that will benefit the employer. Describe how your work has led to measurable outcomes benefiting your organization.

- Is it easy to follow? Keep to a logical pattern, following conventions. With a chronological CV, start with the most recent job and work backwards. Use present tense verbs for your current job, and past tense verbs for all previous jobs.

- Are all the words used in their simplest form? You don't want to make the person doing the shortlisting feel inferior if they don't understand your superabundance of polysyllabic terminology (your use of too many big words!).

Review the layout
It is usually best to stick to the following principles:

- Margins should be at least one inch wide. Don't make smaller margins so you can fit in more words.

- Use bold formatting for your name and section headings and to emphasize key words.

- Use italics for the names of publications and foreign phrases, if any.

- Use just two font sizes, and avoid ALL CAPS and too much underlining.

- Do not justify the text. A ragged right edge is much easier to read.

- Put your name in the footer using a smaller typeface.

- Put the dates on the right-hand side if you want to de-emphasize them.

Read and read again

You must re-read your CV: once for accuracy (numbers, city names, etc.), once for missing/extra words, and then once more for spelling. Don't rely too heavily on a spell-checker; it will not catch misused yet properly spelled words like sun or son, site or sight, form or from, etc.

Check that your CV is free of jargon

We often use abbreviations and acronyms (TQM, ALS, BPR), or internal descriptions for job roles which have little meaning for others. Make sure everything is easy to follow and ask someone else to read your CV to check they understand it.

A final check

Before you send off your CV, go through the following checks:

- Is it achievement-orientated (as opposed to a list of what the job involved)?

- Are the verbs in the 'active' tense? You write 'I did', 'I achieved' rather than e.g. 'I was recognised for'

Active: 'Delivered excellent customer service, leading to company recognition.'

Passive: 'Was recognized for customer service skills.'

- Does it emphasize your special skills?

- Does it emphasize special achievements outside work?

- Have you avoided any 'gaps' which would trouble the interviewer?

- Is what you have done quantified where appropriate? (Interviewers love the use of numbers, e.g. 'How much money/time did you save?'

- Have you used significant or emphasizing adjectives? ('Excellent experience', 'sole responsibility')

- Are you saying what you can do for the employer (focusing on benefits)?

- Are you telling them only what they need to know?

Alternatives to a two-page CV

A CV does not have to be two sides of A4. You could turn it into a tri-fold leaflet, fold it so it fits inside a special occasion card and send this at Easter or Christmas, and so on. If you are a designer you could create a booklet.

If your job involves analysis of numbers, think how best you can create a means of conveying this skill. If you think you are strategic, create a strategic report.

You can see some examples of creative CVs here:

http://pinterest.com/amazingpeople/example-cvs/

I don't expect most people to be able to create CVs exactly like these, but you may be able to take some inspiration.

7. Getting ready for your job search

A job search benefits from being structured and organized. You will have daily, weekly and ad hoc tasks; what's important is that you review how things are going and, if you encounter setbacks, you review so you can learn and move forward. But don't forget to congratulate yourself on your successes too!

You must decide how much time you can devote to your job search. If you are not in work, your job hunt can be your full-time job, but if you are looking for a job while in work, you need to find the time, possibly by getting up earlier or watching less TV. Think about how much time you can realistically devote to your job search – is two hours a day possible?

Not everyone has the luxury of a home office so the first task is to make sure you have space, both on your computer and at home, to keep things safe and easy to access. You will want desk space to work, storage space for paper and documentation and a system so you can easily access ads and applications.

You will want to have both online and paper-based filing systems so you can quickly access relevant copies of your CV, etc. You also need to have all your certificates and diplomas ready, as you often need to show these to confirm your qualifications.

USEFUL TIP

Each time you apply for a job, keep a copy of the job ad, the relevant version of your CV and your cover letter so you can refer to them again. Keeping each in a separate plastic wallet could be helpful. Also keep copies of your correspondence each time you make a direct approach to an organization or agency.

At times you will have to post a letter or application – not everything is done online – so have some good-quality paper available to use.

Have an online or paper system to schedule tasks (daily and weekly 'to do' lists) and keep track of appointments. You should also keep a log of everyone you are contacting and when, to make it easy to follow up.

A daily activity log

Each evening, make a note of what you will do the following day. This will keep you focused and ensure you do the most important tasks first. Your tasks will include people to talk to, jobs to apply for and research to undertake.

List your objectives for the day and make a note of how long you intend to spend on each task. You can later review to make sure you are making good use of your time.

Remember the following when planning your day:

- It can be most productive to do phone calls in a block, perhaps calling at 10–11 am or 2–3 pm.

Example daily activity log:
24th April

- Bought the *Guardian* to scan for jobs. I put a cross through those that were clearly unsuitable and used my highlighter to ring any that would be of interest.

- Visited the library to read the *Financial Times* to keep up on industry changes.

- Chatted to another job hunter and went for a coffee. We swapped cards and will meet in the library next week to pass on any useful information. Glad I have her email details.

- Saw that XXX services are expanding. They may have some upcoming vacancies in my area of expertise; I've made a note to follow up.

- Spent all afternoon on my application form to ABC Ltd; it was a complicated form so I was glad I had photocopied it yesterday so I could use it to create a draft copy.

- Looked at my letter and tweaked it so I could send it to XXX. I rang first to find out who was going to be the most appropriate person to send it to.

- Received a phone call from Colin Pemberton (01606 XXXXXX). He's a friend of Andrew Wilson and said there may be something coming up and he would like to meet. We have arranged to meet at the Old Vicarage, Holmes Chapel at 11.45am this Friday. Forgot to ask for some info on the company but have made a note to do an Internet search.

- Made a note to follow up on the ten letters I sent out last week; this will be my first task tomorrow morning.

- Try to just do one thing at a time and follow it through.

- Make sure to leave some time for the unexpected.

- Don't forget to include lunch breaks and relaxation.

Your activity log will help you recall what you have done and who you have contacted, and will make sure you follow through on each activity.

You can then review at the end of each day to see where time could have been better spent and to remind yourself of all the positive steps you took. Ask yourself:

- What did I do today?

- What was helpful?

- What hindered?

- What one action can I take tomorrow to make a big difference to help me reach my objective of a new job?

Measurement and monitoring is important, so as well as a daily list of tasks, I suggest you measure the following *each week*:

- How many jobs have I applied for which are *a close match* to what I want?

- How many interviews have I had?

- How many job search phone calls have I made?

- How much relevant research have I undertaken?

- How many people have I connected with?

- How many people have I reconnected with?

- How many people have I connected with on LinkedIn?

- How many direct approaches have I made?

- How many professional meetings have I attended?

There is likely to be some activity that you avoid – what is it? Contacting companies direct? Doing in-depth research? Make a note and ask others to help you get past this block.

For next week, target completing a set number of tasks, such as 'I will make 20 networking calls', 'I will do two hours of relevant job search each day', etc. Make a note now of what you will challenge yourself to do.

Challenging yourself to go that bit beyond your comfort zone should result in you doing more than you would normally. To aim for 20 calls and make fifteen is still a success if otherwise you may only have done five. Don't put yourself down. Look to celebrate mini-achievements, with, say, a trip to the cinema after 20 cold calls.

Many times I hear of people who apply for 100+ jobs a week. The only way they can do this is to use a generic CV and submit it with a standard cover letter. They then experience rejection again and again. Stop applying for anything you can remotely do and start focusing on jobs where you match the requirements. Stop wasting your time applying for jobs you have no chance of getting.

Wait until you are interview-ready before you start to apply for jobs. If you 'blow it' with a particular company, it may be harder to be considered for any future jobs that may be on offer.

Use different approaches

There are different ways to get a job: direct and indirect, and proactive and reactive. Look at the diagram below. Too many people focus on the options on the right, when they are most likely to get a job using the options on the left.

	Direct approaches		
Proactive	Speculative approaches	Advertised jobs	Reactive
	Networking	Recruitment agencies	
	Indirect approaches		

Don't fall into the trap of focusing purely on jobs advertised in the press or online. This is the least effective way of finding a job. The best way of finding a job is to use people you know – your network – and to make direct contact with companies you want to work for.

Effective job search approaches

Most effective

↑
Networking
Direct approaches to companies
Fact-finding interviews
Employment agencies
Look at job sites
Look at jobs posted in the paper
↓

Least effective

How are you feeling about your job search?

Judy is feeling excited and enthusiastic about finding a new job. Nilesh is less positive – the words he used were 'scary' and 'depressing'. He said that if he was honest, he would rather go to the dentist than start applying for jobs.

Judy is far more likely to have a positive experience. She knows that the worst that can happen when she sends off her CV is to hear nothing, but she will focus much more on active job search. She knows that being focused on a specific goal will put her well ahead of the competition. Judy is positive and is ready to make direct approaches to organizations and people.

Be *committed*. Take a half-hearted approach and you won't get anywhere. You need to be committed to your success.

81

Get mentally ready

Get those endorphins released. Stand up and close your eyes. Imagine anything that makes you happy, such as success in your job hunt. Then imagine you are successful and enjoying the success. Do this every day.

We must be realistic on how long our job search will take. In a good economy it can take about three months. In an economic downturn it can take twice as long, but it depends on the type of job you seek – there are many more entry- and junior-level positions than senior posts.

If you have been unemployed for a long time, you may already be feeling low and wondering if you will ever get a job. Chapter 16, Staying Motivated, will be helpful but for now it might be good to take your CV off any job boards till you have gone through this book and can then start again re-energized.

Your **locus of control** can affect motivation. Some people have an *internal* locus of control: they consider that they are in control of any decisions they make, rather than being influenced by others. These people know that success in a career is down to them and the actions they take. Other people have an *external* locus of control: they feel that decisions and results are outside of their control – they think that 'what will be will be' and that no matter what they do, it won't affect the outcome.

If you have an external locus of control, spending more time with positive people who believe they will succeed can be helpful – it will help you learn how to take more responsibility for what happens.

Adjusting your goal

You will need a realistic goal. The job you are qualified to do may not be available, or you may not be able to stay on the same career path – no matter how good you are. You may need to think about what else you can and want to do, to refocus skills to suit something else. If you have (or had) a job you hated, this might be the best time to consider alternatives. Check there is a realistic chance you will be successful in the job you seek.

You may think it will be easier to get a job at a lower level than your previous job. But an employer is likely to assume that you will leave as soon as you get a better offer. If you decide to go for a lower-level job, when you apply, you must make it very clear how your background will be of benefit to the organization you are applying to, and that you are not seeking a return to your previous level. The quality of the job is more important to you.

Interviews – you must want the job!

One of my clients emailed with good news: he's got an interview next week. He's not sure if he wants the job but said that he would go along for interview practice. He was found through a site where he had uploaded his CV. He's an experienced procurement manager with masses of experience, but he no longer wants a long commute and would prefer to work for a smaller, more local company in a more 'operations-focused' role.

So this job doesn't meet his requirements. It's going to be back in central London, he'll have a three-hour daily commute and he's not sure he wants to work for this particular company – he knows the culture isn't a good match for him.

I asked him why he was going for the interview and he said that it was for interview practice. I strongly advised against this. When we go for interview we must want the job we apply for, otherwise we are setting ourselves up for rejection.

If we really want the job, we will do lots of research and preparation, we will carefully research topics they might ask us about, we will think hard about how we really match up with the job spec and we will diligently list questions we could ask.

If we aren't committed, our preparation will be half-hearted, but most importantly, we will be unlikely to come across as someone committed and interested in this particular job and the result will be rejection. Why set ourselves up to fail? Far better to use the time to go for something we do want to do.

The best approach is to only apply for jobs you actually want. If you get approached, decide if you want the job, or would take it if offered. If you answer yes then give 100 per cent to your preparation; if not, politely decline.

8. Creating your message – the pitch

Friends and people you meet will ask you what you are looking for. What are you going to tell them? If you are vague, you've missed a chance to get people on your side, helping you identify relevant contacts and possible job openings. We need a short message which makes it very clear what we want – our 30-second pitch.

This pitch is sometimes called a 'personal commercial' or an 'elevator speech', as you will take about the same amount of time as in a TV or radio commercial, or if you were travelling in a lift (although you may get some strange looks if you just launch into this next time you are in a lift!).

James says, 'I don't mind what I do, I just want a job', but this makes it hard for people to help. Christina, on the other hand, is clear on what she is looking for:

My name is Christina Woodcock and I'm an experienced sales manager. I thoroughly enjoy managing people, building relationships and problem-solving, and would love to find a role that allows me to further develop these skills.

Other good examples of 30-second pitches are: 'I've worked as a legal executive and now want to move into public relations'; 'I've been an occupational therapist, but am now looking for a job which will use my written communication skills such as for a newspaper, a magazine, or company newsletter'; 'I'm looking for a job working with children in places like a nursery school, day care, hospital, or primary school.'

These examples are specific rather than general. Rather than say something like 'I'm looking for something in the training field', it is more effective to say something like 'I'm a technical trainer looking for opportunities to teach end-users how to use business applications software in a Windows environment.' This will really help people to help you.

The format of a pitch needs to be in clear stages, such as:

- Who I am and my expertise
- What I do and how I can help
- What I need

Let's look at these stages in more detail:

The 'Who I am' and 'my expertise' stage
The first step is to say who you are and what you do, for example: 'Hello, I'm David Pearson and I'm an expert in supply chain management.'

You should ideally introduce yourself as an expert in a particular area. You could say:

I'm _____ and my expertise is in _____

My name is _____. I'm a specialist _____

I'm _____. I'm specially trained in _____

My name is _____. I'm a qualified _____

This needs to be upbeat and positive. You don't want to come across as negative, so don't say things such as 'I'm Fred Jones and I've been made redundant' or 'I'm Christine Lewis and I'm an unemployed graduate'.

The 'What I do' and the 'how I can help' phase

The second step is to say **what you do**, or **how you help**. This helps people to understand the detail of your work. A job title is too distant. Do people really know what it means? People may know your job title but not what it entails and not your specific talents and accomplishments, so make it clear, for example:

I work with teams to ensure that the supply lines in place run smoothly, so customers come back time after time for their goods. I want to use my diverse skills such as xxx and yyy to contribute to organisational success.

Some other examples include:

I **create** warm relationships with customers so they come back and buy from me again and again.

I am **careful** with my deliveries and make it a smooth and pleasant transaction for customers.

The 'What I need' stage

The final part is to say what you need from them. If you want people to help on your career quest you need to be specific. If you say, 'I am looking for a well-paid job', or 'I need security for the future', it is far too broad, while saying 'I was a child care worker' isn't specific about what you *want*.

Others may say, 'I'm looking to talk with people who can help me get a better understanding of the role of technical author' or 'I would like to explore the possibility of working as a TV researcher. Would you know someone who I could talk with?' or 'I'm looking for professionals to talk with to discuss how to make the transition from marketing to finance. Could you suggest someone for me to talk to?'

Create your own 30-second pitch and write it down.

Say it aloud. Does it flow? Does it sound right for you? It should sound natural so use less formal language. Say it aloud to family and friends and be receptive to feedback. Make any changes you need to make and write it down again.

Roger David was clear what he wanted and prepared what to say:

My name is David and I've 15 years experience in supply chain management. I've worked in procurement management for 2 blue chip companies including time spent in China and Germany. I'm now seeking a fresh challenge with a company that adds value to its customers' supply chains and has innovative products in a growing market. Do you know who I might speak with to explore opportunities that may exist within XXXX Group?

This led to several people helping him get in touch with others and, later, success at interview.

You can use your pitch any time you are in contact with people who you think might be able to help you in your job search. It is versatile enough to be used in different ways, for example:

- At interview, to answer the question 'Tell me about yourself'

- In a cover letter to highlight your background and key abilities

- When talking to people to help you get contacts for fact-finding interviews

- At any event when you are asked to introduce yourself

- When cold-calling companies to explain how you may be of service

- As part of your LinkedIn summary.

Now you have learnt how to create this, you can keep your pitch up to date as you develop into new roles.

9. LinkedIn

Alongside your CV you also need to be on LinkedIn. Whilst there are a range of social media you could use (Facebook, Twitter, Pinterest ...), it is LinkedIn that will be most effective in achieving success in your job search.

With over 10 million people on LinkedIn in the UK, and well over 178 million worldwide, it's the place to be found, but it is also a giant search engine and can be an effective part of researching and networking.

To use it effectively, you must have a completed profile, with photo, recommendations and connections. Too many people start to complete their profile, leave it half-finished without even a photo, and are then negative about it, saying it doesn't work. But that's like submitting a half-completed CV for a job and then wondering why you haven't been shortlisted. Or joining a gym and wondering why you haven't got any fitter – you need to do the work!

Having a profile on LinkedIn means that you can be found by recruiters, and also allows you to connect with other people who work in the field you want to work in – you can ask questions, exchange information and find out about opportunities.

How recruiters use LinkedIn

LinkedIn is a cost-effective way for recruiters to find people. They will enter their criteria, such as accountants within a

50-mile radius of Northampton with experience working for light engineering companies. If you meet these criteria, you will appear in their shortlist. Without a photo they'll probably move on by and you won't even have your profile reviewed. Get through that and they'll do a quick review, paying attention to any recommendations you have. Recruiters also search for specific skills, so you should have relevant skills listed on your CV, and also get endorsements from people who recognize your skills.

Getting started

The time to start is now. It's far better to get connecting and discussing with others before you need their help. Set up an account at linkedin.com and add all relevant details: current situation, company, job title and postcode. You will be asked to connect your email account to start connecting with people. I suggest you skip this step, and wait until you have got your profile completed – you don't want people coming to your profile when there is hardly any information entered.

Adding more detail

You have 120 characters to create a professional headline, so make good use of them. This professional headline will be included each time you appear on LinkedIn: it appears as a status update, when you ask or answer a question – so you want it to stand out.

There are many ways you can write your headline, and you can change it whenever you like. You could say something as short as 'Management Accountant' but would that capture the attention of a recruiter? Think of the difference if you wrote something like, 'I save money for professional services firms by reviewing and improving processes.'

As LinkedIn is being used more and more as a search engine, you may prefer to use a list of key words to increase your chances of being found through a search. This is a new technique, pioneered by career coaches, so for example mine, using 120 characters, is:

Award Winning Career Coach | Author 'How to Get a Job in a Recession' | Career Coaching | Job Search | Personal Branding

Photo

Upload a photo. Without one you will significantly reduce your chances of people connecting with you. Critically review the photos you have and choose a professional, head-and-shoulders shot, where people get a good view of your face and especially your eyes.

Summary

You have up to 2,000 characters for your summary. What you write should be clear, focused on your objective and should take about 30 seconds to read out loud. Write in the first person – it should come across as if you are talking to the reader. You can use paragraphs and symbols such as ~~ or ** to break up the text.

The summary is different to your CV, but the message should be consistent. Include highlights from your career history and also strengths you can offer an employer. You will have key words in your CV; use these same key words in your LinkedIn profile so you are more likely to appear on a shortlist when employers are searching for people with a particular skill set.

LinkedIn is different to a CV. We aren't constrained by a two-page layout and can write up our background and desires in a more market-focused way. The main objective should be to make it compelling.

Career history

You can include all the jobs you have had, but you don't need to go into great detail. Again include key words and avoid company acronyms that lack meaning to others.

Additional information

There are optional sections for detailing group projects, honours and awards, involvement in organizations, test scores and courses. List your skills and certifications, courses you have undertaken, and projects; these can be particularly useful for university students and recent graduates. You could also include details of your interests. The link to add sections is just below the shaded main section.

You can also include links to three websites. If you have had an article published you could add a link to this. You don't need to use all three but this is the only place to include a hyperlink so it's well worth using if you can. Most people use the default 'My Blog' or 'My Website' but you can change these to include the actual name of your blog or a more accurate description, such as 'My article on XXX published in *People Management*' or 'Denise Taylor's personal website'. If you have a Twitter account you can include a link to your Twitter page.

Claim your name!
The default URL is a less-than-memorable mix of numbers and letters. This is very difficult for you and others to remember. But you may be able to use your name. Whilst mine is quite a common name, I was able to get http://uk.linkedin.com/in/denisetaylor. If this hadn't been available I would have included my middle initial or perhaps added MBA after my name.

Privacy settings
Check and make sure you are comfortable with your privacy settings. You do this via the 'Account & Settings' tab at the top of your profile. Make sure that your 'public profile' is set to display full profile information so that it's accessible to search engines. You can choose, for example, not to have

your data shared with third-party applications, and whether you want advertising messages to be sent to you.

Seeking groups

There are over 500,000 groups on LinkedIn. Search for those that relate to your company, industry, school or career interests. You can join a maximum of 50 groups and this is a great way to make contacts and develop relationships. It's difficult to deal with the sheer number of updates for a large number of groups but you can opt for a daily digest or a 'no email' option. A benefit of joining a number of groups is that it increases the number of people you are connected with.

Groups include:

- Industry-specific groups
- Trade and professional groups
- Employer alumni groups
- University groups
- Career-related groups
- Functional groups
- Personal interest groups

Each group will operate slightly differently: some will automatically grant you access; with others your application will be reviewed. Each group includes links to discussions, news, jobs and sometimes subgroups.

Groups are a great place to ask questions but also answer questions and respond to posts. This will raise your profile. Perhaps choose just two groups that you will get involved with on at least a weekly basis – better to start small and build up than to get overwhelmed.

Save and publicize

You can save a PDF version of your profile so you can read it offline. I recommend you read it alongside your CV; is the message consistent? Do the dates match up? Once you are happy, you can start to publicize your LinkedIn profile via a link on your CV, email signature, business card and in any professional directories.

Getting ready to connect

You need to get the basics ready before attempting to connect with people – you want to come across as efficient (I would expect!) and interesting, so use this checklist.

- Is your profile focused on the sort of job you are looking for?

- Have you identified and included relevant key words for this job in your tagline/summary/specialities?

- Have you included your location?

- Do you have a compelling headline? Don't copy someone else's; make it personal.

- Do you have a professional photo that focuses on your head and shoulders? People want to be able to see your eyes!

- Have you personalized your URL to make it easier to pass on details to others? You can then include this on your CV and in your email signature.

- Is your summary compelling and easy to read? Does it showcase your key achievements? Would you want to get in touch with you?

- Have you included details on your current and past experience? Include at least a short summary of each job. A recruiter may want to meet someone who has worked for a particular organization, so be sure to name them.

- Have you include specialities and added top skills? You can include up to 50 skills.

- Have you included education, projects, courses etc.?

- Do you have recommendations? Start by giving them to other people, people may then recommend you.

- Have you joined relevant groups? Join groups which are relevant to what you are looking for. Where do the key players for your profession hang out?

Status update box

This allows you to provide details of what you are working on: for example, an event you are presenting at or attending, a significant accomplishment at work, a blog post or article you have published. Aim to update at least a couple of times a week.

Seeking connections

You are now ready to connect with people. You can search your email account and connect with people you know. Please don't send out the default message – instead, choose a personal message that demonstrates some thought.

You can then search for people you used to work with or met at school or university; it might be interesting to see what they are doing now. You can also look through the collection of business cards you have accumulated and connect with the people who gave the cards to you.

Once you have connected with the people you already know, you can seek to connect with 'second-level contacts', the people who your contacts know.

Research using LinkedIn

If you want to apply for a job within a particular company but don't know who to contact, then you need to find someone who can help you. You can use LinkedIn to find people who work, or have worked, for a particular company and send them a message. It doesn't even have to be someone in the department you want to work in – often contacting someone from a different department can be just as useful. For example, if you are an electrical engineer, you can make contact with an accountant at that company and ask them questions. You can say something like:

> I'm really interested in working with XYZ Company as an electrical engineer. Would you be able to suggest the right person for me to talk with about this career path?

Or

> As someone who has worked with XYZ Organization for four years, can you suggest ways I could make a speculative application stand out from many others?

Or

> I have an interview scheduled next week with XYZ Company – could you let me know more about what it's like to work with your company and, in particular, details about the company culture?

As you research organizations that interest you, review individual profiles. You may see that people in the jobs you aspire to all belong to a specific professional association; if so, join a relevant LinkedIn group. It's a great way to connect with people.

Look up people who work for the organization that interests you and note where they previously worked. You could also look up people who have moved on from that organization, and find out where they moved to – it could provide interesting career paths to review.

You may feel uncomfortable making contact with someone currently working for the organization and who you barely know; people who used to work for the organization are another option. They may be more willing to talk openly about what it is really like to work there.

Recommendations

People pay attention to recommendations, and you should seek these out from people you have worked with in the past. You could tell them the sort of job you are looking for and your key attributes, skills and achievements, so they can write with this in mind. Recommendations don't have to be long, and you may find that past bosses and colleagues are happy to write a recommendation.

If it has been a while you could remind them of your achievements and personal qualities. Also recommend others – be specific in what you say. Your recommendation will then appear on both your profile and theirs.

If you are being made redundant, ask your manager for a recommendation before you leave. The recommendation will let other people know that you were valued. You could also seek recommendations from clients if you are connected to them. As the manager, you can also ask for a recommendation from your team, possibly focused on your leadership qualities.

Networking on LinkedIn
Earlier I suggested you identify some groups to join, but joining is not enough; you need to be an active participant. Raise your profile by answering questions, or share information by posting links to articles, with a reason why others should read them.

Introductions

You may be very keen to contact someone who is not part of your network. If that person is connected to someone you know, you can ask for them to introduce you. However, just because a person is a first-level contact with someone, it doesn't mean that they know them well, so if they decline to help, it's probably not down to anything you have done.

When asking for an introduction, create a short email that they can then send on to the person you want to connect with. Write it as if it is from them, so that the changes they need to make are minimal. Draw out your achievements and include details to make somebody feel compelled to connect to you.

You can also use InMail. If you have opted for the premium (paid) service you can send messages to anyone, whether you are connected or not.

Make LinkedIn part of a weekly routine

You can't complete your profile and think that's it! At least a couple of times a week, update your status, read updates from your connections, read and comment on discussions within groups you belong to, review your connections, see what they are doing and how you can help, identify jobs to apply for, and use LinkedIn to help with research.

What about other social media?

I've concentrated on LinkedIn as this is the most important social media to use. You could also consider Twitter, Pinterest and Facebook.

10. Making applications

So many people end up with rejection letters because of a poor technique. They see a job they think they can do, then send off their CV and a brief note without spending much effort on targeting their application.

Having some structure will greatly increase your chances of success. I'm going to explain exactly what you need to do – you will follow the same process I share with my clients.

Step 1: Find the vacancies

Create a shortlist of the sites which best meet your particular needs. If you are a finance manager, you are likely to find that different sites are better for you than if you were an account executive or a technical writer.

Don't waste time surfing around many sites; get focused and identify the right ones for you. Don't forget about smaller niche sites; you will want to make sure these are included in the aggregator, and if not to add them to your 'to do' list and LinkedIn – it can cost a lot of money to advertise on the major sites, so it is much more cost-effective for organizations to choose a more targeted means of advertising.

When you register on these websites you can get job details sent direct to your inbox. Be too vague in your requirements and you will be inundated, so focus on your targeted job area.

Look at different job aggregator sites such as Indeed, available in 50+ countries and 26 languages, and SimplyHired, available in 17 countries. The main reason to use an aggregator is that it brings together the results from many different job sites, newspaper job sections, company career pages, recruitment agencies and more. It will also save you a great deal of time. But you must set clear parameters so you aren't swamped with job suggestions.

Not all advertised jobs exist. Some agencies trawl for CVs and there is no specific job, so don't build your hopes up.

You need to be mindful of identity theft, so before you upload your details make sure you can conceal your identity and protect your contact information. When you start using online sites, keep track of the level of privacy you chose for your CV and/or contact information. Also print out the **Privacy Policy** and **Terms of Use** on the date you first used the site, and monitor these for changes on a regular basis.

Ensure that you can edit your CV to suit different jobs and that you are able to delete your CV when you have found a job. You don't want your new employer to think you are unhappy and looking for another job. With some sites, you can upload more than one version of your CV, which is helpful if you have a few jobs that you are interested in.

In this case, make a note of which version is uploaded and where.

Searching on job sites takes up time but is not efficient job hunting. You shouldn't spend more than about 20 per cent of your available time identifying jobs to apply for; you need to spend much more time on research and meeting people.

Step 2: Review the job ad

Applying properly for a job takes time, so focus more on jobs where you are a close match. An effective approach is to:

- Review the job ads and identify those where you closely match the requirements.

- Print out then highlight the key points in the job ad.

- Compare your skills and experience with those required. Confirm that you are a close or perfect match.

- Go beyond the job ad to consider what else may enhance your application. You may have skills which may not be specified in the advert but could be of interest to the prospective employer.

In a buoyant market you could apply for jobs where you don't fully match, but when there are many applicants, employers want a close match. Before you dive into an in-depth and comprehensive application, make sure that you can provide specific examples of how you meet the job requirements.

USEFUL TIP

The closing date may change, so don't be caught out. A job ad may be taken down early if the organization decide they already have enough applications. Be ready to apply by having standard passages you can cut and paste into a job application and then customize to a particular job.

A simple way to confirm you meet the job requirements is to create two columns. Put the requirements from the ad on the left and your examples on the right. For example, if the ad says 'self-starter', refer to examples of where you have taken the initiative. It could look something like the table shown opposite.

You can use this research to adapt your CV for this particular job and to write the cover letter. You would put more detail in an actual letter, but this analysis will show you where you are strong and where you lack expertise.

Step 3: Gather relevant information

Some ads are very brief, so be proactive and phone the organization to find out more about the job. It's not 100 per cent certain that you will get to speak with someone, but be positive and try to speak to the recruiter. Do have your accomplishments ready in case you are asked questions.

Their needs	My experience/skills
Over 7 years' experience of working in a customer focused environment	Nearly 5 years in prestigious serviced office environment 3½ of which spent in a **managerial role** in charge of front of house and customer service teams
Proven successful track record of training and motivating staff	Reduced staff turnover and increased number of internal promotions by building empowered, goal-driven teams; created and implemented staff training and development programme; maintained high staff morale and a cooperative working environment; coached and mentored underperformers; rewarded exceptional performance
Proven HR experience to carry out disciplinaries and appraisals	Conducted regular performance reviews and annual appraisals; obtained 360 degree feedback; created and implemented individual and team performance plans; carried out disciplinary procedures
High customer focus	Achieved on average 95 per cent customer satisfaction; increased client retention to over 90 per cent; formally recognised for delivering excellent service

If the relevant person is not available to speak to you, ask for the job description and person specification. These will help you to create your cover letter and adapt your CV, or to help with completing an application form. You can then continue comparing your experience and skills with the requirements.

The sorts of questions you should ask include:

- What is the exact job title?

- Who does the person report to?

- What specific experience are you looking for?

- What are the most important tasks that will need to be done?

- What factors would cause a candidate to be eliminated from consideration?

- Is this a new position? If not, what happened to the previous job holder?

- What qualifications are essential?

- Are there specific problems you will want the new employee to solve?

Alas, you may not always get more information, so use the research you undertook as you considered what jobs to apply for.

You have already demonstrated you match up through the two-column approach, so now you can focus on your application. You will need to review and revise your CV or complete an application, and to write a cover letter, or use the 'further information' section on an application form, to explain your suitability for the job.

Step 4: Revise your CV

You have a master CV but will need to adapt it for a particular job. You have highlighted key requirements in the job ad; now review your CV to see if you can enhance any of the achievement bullets to be more focused on the job requirements. If the job description requires someone with great organizational skills, highlight on your CV a job or a project in which you demonstrated your strengths in organization. If it stresses the need for leadership qualities, you must include an example of a time when you displayed leadership skills.

An ad may request 'five years' sales experience in computer or related industry'. Look again at your achievement bullets and include as many of these key words as possible. If you have previous experience as an area sales manager, you can expand it to say 'six years' experience as area sales manager for computers, laptops and printers'. Read through your CV with fresh eyes and make sure that as many of the examples as possible relate to this particular job.

Consider the size of the organization and again adapt your examples. If applying to a large organization, highlight your experience working for large organizations; for a small organization, show how you can transfer your skills to a niche player, how you can work in a small team and how you are happy to muck in when there is pressure on time.

Throughout, try to match your application to the advertised position and show that you really do want this particular job with this organization. Use phrases corresponding to key words in the job advertisement or expressions that show that you know something about the organization and its products and services.

When submitting an application via an online portal, shortlisting will be done through your use of key words, but once you get through this stage, your letter will be reviewed. Other organizations still review each application on an individual basis. Help the recruiter by showing them how you match up. Creating your cover letter will be dealt with in the next chapter.

Application forms

Most people prefer to submit a CV and cover letter/email, but many organizations, especially in the public sector, prefer application forms. Application forms make it quick and easy for an organization to compare applications from a number of different people as the information is presented in a standard way.

Application forms vary in length and will include factual information about you and about your education, career, health and interests. They will usually include open-ended questions about your reasons for applying for the job and the contribution that you think you can make.

You may think it a lot more work – and it will be for the first application form you complete – but save all the detail in a Word document and you should be able to edit and use it again in future applications.

The basics

Read the instructions carefully before you start. Make sure you understand what information is needed and where. Always keep in mind the particular requirements of the job for which you are applying. That is why the initial analysis is so helpful.

Some application forms are Word documents you can save offline, complete and then email, but many are completed online. You can still type offline to ensure that your responses are grammatically correct, without typos, and then copy and paste in the details later.

With an online form, the text boxes for you to type in may be fixed (and you may have a set number of words or characters to use) or they may expand to include unlimited information. If you are given, for example, 100 words for your reply, aim to be as close as possible to the word limit.

Some questions will require brief, factual answers. Others will seek a narrative answer; this should be drafted and redrafted so that it is as good as it can be.

Additional information (also known as the personal statement)

Usually there is a section for you to provide further information in support of your application. This is often the section that interviewers read most carefully.

Make sure you include information on *why* you want the job and *what* makes you the right candidate. Wherever you can, bring out your strengths, skills and achievements, and not only the responsibilities that you have.

Strengthen your application in such sections by stating a key reason for being considered for the job and backing it up immediately with an example. If possible, use terms from the advertisement for your main reasons; continue for two or three key points, substantiating each general statement with an example. This can make your application very persuasive and penetrating.

Be positive and only include negative points if essential. For example, you can't lie about the amount of time you have had off sick but you don't need to mention any lowlights of your career such as crises of confidence, substantial errors of judgement, etc.

 Imagine you are asked at interview 'Why should we appoint you?' Your answer to that question could be all the things to be brought out in the open-ended section.

Competency-based questions

Some application forms will ask you to provide details about your experience in some specific areas against a number of headings. These are likely to be the competencies you are assessed on throughout the selection process, so you must provide very clear examples. Such forms may appear complicated but are a structured approach to selling yourself through the application process. Once you understand the structure you can also use this with interview preparation.

The competencies included will have been identified by the employer through the job analysis process, and will be key skills or personal qualities needed for the job. The questions generally include some guidance, such as:

For each scenario you are asked to describe a situation (ideally fairly recent) from your own experience, which you think is the best example of what you have done and which demonstrates the specified ability.

Another organization has the following bullet points:

For each scenario you should:

- *Briefly outline the situation*
- *Describe what you actually did*
- *Say what the outcome was and give your estimate of the proportion of credit you can claim for that outcome*
- *Say what you gained from the experience.*

Your answer can draw on your experiences in any kind of setting, e.g. paid employment, education, voluntary work or leisure activities. Let's look at a couple of examples.

Describe an effective team of which you are a member. What is your particular contribution to the team? In what way is the team effective?

'I have been a member of a local cricket club for the last two years, which is not only fun but also gets me out from behind a desk. I am an important member of the team as I am the main strike bowler and a sound middle-order batsman with an average of over 20 last season, and I was therefore partially responsible for one of the club's most successful seasons in its history. In addition to good performances on the field, the club also performed well off the field, as we organized various fundraising events that have benefited both the club and the community. For example, this year we held a fête where I was responsible for running a food stall, which improved my organizational and interpersonal skills.'

Describe a situation where you had to persuade someone to do something. How did you go about it? Were you successful?

'During the Duke of Edinburgh Award scheme I led a group that improved the habitats and facilities of the Country Park at Marbury, Cheshire. It was often necessary to motivate a member of the team to start a new project or work in unfavourable weather conditions for example. Past experience of captaining the school rifle-shooting and tennis teams has shown me that the most effective method of persuading someone to do something was to confront them and persuade them of the wisdom of my proposals. There was an instance during the Duke of Edinburgh Award scheme where a person did not want to begin the construction of a footpath as it was getting late. As his participation was essential and his negativity could have had a damaging effect on group morale, I drew on past experiences and persuaded him to continue working and the group made excellent progress.'

The following examples are in a slightly different style but also require you to be specific in the way you respond. It can help to use the STAR acronym.

STAR

First describe the **Situation**, then the **Task** you had to do. Follow up with the **Action** you took and then the **Result**.

Motivation

You will need to be intellectually curious, interested in the work, interested in international affairs, gain satisfaction from the nature of the work itself, behave with integrity and honesty in all matters, and be a self-starter, committed to developing skills and abilities. Please give an example where you have demonstrated these abilities.

'While teaching English in Prague, I regularly attended teaching workshops presented by more experienced teachers. These workshops were highly interesting as they provided new ideas and methods for teaching English and were a valuable source of inspiration.

'After attending a workshop on using the news as a source of discussion I organized a debate around the theme of immigration in one of my advanced groups. There were two teams; one had to argue against immigration, another in favour of it. I was the judge/moderator of the discussion.

'This exercise went well as both teams became extremely involved in the discussion and I was pleased by the quality of their arguments and the English they used.'

Resilience

You will need to be able to cope with conflicting demands, be prepared to undertake the mundane as well as the challenging, be able to work under pressure, to deal with stress, to work long hours, cope with criticism, be robust, patient and able to cope with frustrations.

'During the final year of my degree, I had to complete a 5,000-word dissertation in addition to the normal course requirements. This additional project meant that I had to work especially hard to co-ordinate my timetable and meet all the demands on my time.

'At the start of the year I planned a detailed timetable, planning all my lectures, project deadlines and other commitments. I also included research time for my dissertation. Throughout the year I followed this timetable, adapting it as necessary in response to changing circumstances. After the first semester, I saw my advisor and was able to respond to his criticisms of my dissertation, which forced me to adapt some of my ideas to incorporate new materials. To meet the dead-line I worked hard redrafting and typing my project.

'At the end of the year I received a high grade for my dissertation and still had enough time to complete my revision before the exam term began.'

Unusual questions

Some companies ask questions that are a bit out of the ordinary. For example, apply for a job with Innocent and you will be asked to respond to the following:

You'd never know it but I can …
You need to write something quirky to make you stand out.

Tell us your reasons for wanting to work at Innocent and the role in question.
Why is this the right job for you … Link answer to details of the job.

We love meeting people who leave things a bit better than they find them. So please tell us about a recent situation where you took the initiative and made something happen …
This is a place to provide a competency-based reply.

We're looking for people who face challenges head on and deliver against the odds. What achievement are you most proud of?
Think of a specific example and be sure to include WHY.

We're especially interested in the stuff that you are passionate about, the things that make you tick. What gets you excited? *What does get you excited? How can you relate this to the job you are applying for?*

Questions are often included to see how you think and to see if you are willing to step outside the answers most will give. The best way to answer questions is to make good use of your background but make it relevant to the organization. In the case of applying for a job, look through the company website and find out as much as you can about their culture and style so examples can be chosen that are likely to suit the organizational norms.

Submitting an application form

Remember, if the form asks you not to send a CV with it, don't. Follow all instructions to the letter.

Check that your answers on the application form mirror information on your CV and LinkedIn profile.

When you have completed the application form, check it very carefully before you hit the 'submit' button.

Submitting CVs and applications via email

When submitting a CV or job application by email, treat it just like a written approach with a proper letter, not just a short email saying 'Here is my CV'. Include details such as job title, reference number, name etc.

When attaching your CV, do not name the file 'CV', how will the recruiter find this again? It is much better to name it, for example, 'DtaylorCV' or even better 'DTaylor_Projectmgt_expert'.

Also, review the email address you use. Too many send applications from the fun/jokey address they use for communicating with friends such as 2JDandcokes@yahoo.com or drunkencow@gmail.com. Keep these for your personal contacts, and for work use a more formal email address such as dk.taylor@gmail.com.

Also avoid emoticons; they do not create a business-orientated impression and may lead to your message being considered spam.

Making contact

If you know someone who works for the company you want to work for, they could deliver your CV direct to the desk of the person doing the shortlisting, with a personal recommendation. Your CV will get much more than the usual cursory glance. (This is unlikely to work in a public sector organization as they usually have a 'no canvassing' rule.)

Applying via agencies

Remember, recruitment agencies work for the employer, who pays their fees. You are a commodity. If they can make money from you, they will be in touch. Some like shorter CVs; others prefer more detailed ones, so pay attention to their requirements. If they ask you to format your CV in a particular way, do it! They may like to present all their candidates in a 'house style'.

Ask them to tell you when they submit your CV for a job to keep track of who has your CV.

11. Cover letters

The cover letter is just as important as your CV. You want it to capture and express your capability and enthusiasm and make the reader want to read your CV. You can either include the cover letter within the body of the email (which makes it easy for the reader to skim) or attach a letter with a similar style (font, contact details) to your CV, thus creating a 'matching pair'.

It is important to take the time to create a letter in which you clearly demonstrate how you match the job requirements; this will increase your chances of being shortlisted. Focus on what you can offer and your enthusiasm for the job rather than what you can get from it.

Expand on your research to create your letter. In Chapter 10, 'Making applications', I suggested that as preparation you match your experience against the organization's requirements through a two-column approach. When you create your cover letter you could use the same approach or turn each requirement into a short paragraph or bullet point.

Your letter should be adapted for each job you apply for and should emphasize your positive assets – education and experience, skills, accomplishments, personal qualities – in relation to the employer's needs. Link your achievements to the job ad. It's fine if you have also included them on your CV.

You will have researched the company as part of your preparation, so when explaining why you are interested in the organization or position, avoid general statements like 'I am impressed with your products and growth.' Write specifically about what products, what growth, and why.

Do not state that you are redundant or bored with your present position – you are seeking a new challenge and this job you are applying for is it!

End the letter with a specific statement of what your next step will be. If you plan to follow up with a phone call, say so. If you plan to wait for the employer's response, say so.

Before you submit your letter, pay attention to details. You can't rely on a spellchecker; too many people send things out with, for example, 'form' instead of 'from'. Lengthy paragraphs are overwhelming to read; divide text into several paragraphs when necessary to keep them short.

Let's move straight on to how to structure your cover letter. This model should help you create an effective accompaniment to your CV.

Remember the following when preparing the relevant sections of your letter:

Name of the person you are writing to

You must make it personal and include the person's name, even if it wasn't included in the job ad. Demonstrate some initiative by tracking down the name of the person you should write to. Do your research on Google or LinkedIn, or call the receptionist.

Opening paragraph

You should always have a strong opening sentence focused on your strengths for this job. You could also indicate how you heard of the position.

Make it exciting, and personal. You want them to know that this letter is being sent just to them and not to a hundred other companies.

Middle paragraph(s)

Your goal here is to show how you can be useful to this particular organization – make it clear why they should shortlist you.

Describe what strengths you have to offer this employer by showing the relationship between your skills and experience and the requirements of the vacant role. You can also describe your previous achievements and how they relate to the role, and identify three reasons why you should be called for interview. It can help to make it very obvious; list the job requirements and, paragraph by paragraph, show how you match up.

Refer the reader to your enclosed/attached CV for additional information.

You can divide this into a couple of smaller paragraphs rather than have one large, dense paragraph.

Closing paragraph

End your letter by clarifying what will happen next. Reiterate your enthusiasm for the job. Plus show some connection to the person reading it, wishing them well in their search for the right person, for example – it's a bit more personal than 'I look forward to hearing from you'!

The process for creating a great cover letter

Once you find a job you want to apply for, go through the ad and highlight all key terms and words. If you get additional information such as a job and person spec you will have further information to review.

You should have done this already as you were getting ready to make an application, and this was covered in Chapter 10, 'Making applications'. You will now review your preparation to create the cover letter.

Pick out what is key. Occasionally you may find as many as 20-plus key criteria, far too many for you to address using the approach I'm going to share, so you have to stick with what is key. Usually these are the ones that will have been included in the job ad.

It can be tempting to want to address every one of the criteria, but imagine how you would feel faced with a 4-page cover letter, you must be targeted on what's key. This leads to the recruitment consultant or HR Manager feeling overwhelmed and your application heading for the bin.

Ideally you will have a named person to write to so you end your letter with 'Yours sincerely'. When you have to write 'Dear Sir or Madam' use 'Yours faithfully'.

Let's now look at a few letters, both of which resulted in the people getting shortlisted.

---

5 Nov 2012

Name
Job Title
Company Name
Address

Dear (Find name),

Project Manager, Brackley, Job Ref xxxx

I am interested in applying for the advertised position, BECAUSE >>> ADD DETAIL ON WHY THIS JOB AND WHY THIS COMPANY. I believe my range of skills and experience will enable me to be successful in this role. Specific aspects of my background that match well with the requirements are:

- **Business Experience:** Have taken full responsibility for all aspects of the daily running of a business, *working autonomously* without local supervision. This included performing *all aspects of customer service* as well as

(continued)

---

maintaining relationships with agents and other organisations including suppliers. The role included taking full responsibility for providing activities for several large corporate events, as well as working with external suppliers to procure appropriate equipment and perform maintenance.

- **Computer Literacy and Numeracy:** Developed and performed research in a highly technical environment, using statistical understanding to analyse large data sets, and have experience of a wide variety of different software packages and operating systems.

- **Organisational skills:** Demonstrated both in my experience of running a business and during another role involving training adult clients, in which I ran classes of up to 15 alone or within a small team. This required a high level of organisation and multi-tasking to monitor and assist the progress of people with widely varying needs. A high level of attention to detail was also demonstrated in assessing work in this role.

My CV provides more detail; I trust my details are of interest and I look forward to hearing from you regarding this application.

Yours sincerely

Dear Samantha

I enclose completed forms as requested. I have also included details of my skills and attributes against your key headings.

I have extensive experience of audit type work, gained through business excellence assessment which involved working as a member of a 7-person team to gain evidence against the 9 areas of the business excellence model. I would analyse the information and produce a report. I also undertook audits to measure the effectiveness of Royal Mail delivery units against three key areas – customer, employee, operational.

Analytical
Through MSc and MBA studies; project management and production of reports.

Inspiring
I am seen as an effective team leader through direct team management and also through leadership of a network of occasional tutors, all senior managers, who, at the time, were all senior in organisational rank to me.

Focused
This was needed to complete my MBA studies. I work best when there are clear goals to be achieved. I am seen as enthusiastic and very much a 'glass half full' personality.

(continued)

Fluent

I am noted for my avoidance of technical jargon and my ability to communicate in an easy to understand way.

Visionary

I can think and operate strategically, via MBA studies and senior management roles.

People Focused

I am noted for my empathy. I am a trained counsellor and work sensitively with others, also taking account of business aims.

I trust you find my details of interest and I'll call on Thursday to discuss further.

Dear Roger

I am very interested in the position of Manufacturing Manager (Ref.) as advertised in the xxxxxx xxxxxxxxxxxxxx and enclose my CV.

I have taken the time to list your specific requirements and my applicable skills in these areas. I hope this will enable you to use your time effectively today.

(continued)

Your key criteria	My background
Work with the Manufacturing Director	Extensive experience of working with board members and managers.
Develop and implement manufacturing strategy	Involved in planning of company strategy
Prepare budget and monitor and control performance against it.	Worked with MD on setting budgets, tracked them monthly against targets
A good communicator with considerable man management skills	Liaised with customers and agents to maximize outputs and profits
Team work/flexible culture	Strong training focus combined with being a team builder
Graduate calibre	HNC in mechanical production engineering plus a range of management development courses
5 years of a modern manufacturing environment	In excess of 5 years' experience

Please do not hesitate to contact me if there is any further information you require.

I look forward to hearing from you.

Yours sincerely

Salary questions

Never mention salary unless specifically asked to. It may be 'too high' or 'too low' and provide an excuse to screen you out. Leave discussion on your package until much later in the selection process. Where you are asked specifically to state salary, either current or expected, you could use a phrase such as 'to be discussed at interview'.

Do bear in mind, however, that some recruiters may view this as unhelpful and be less inclined to see you as a result. So you need to make the final decision yourself.

Salary quotes can be based on many different things, and nowadays some companies will give you a choice of using some of your salary to pay for a car, private healthcare etc. So if you are concerned about your present salary being some way below the level you are aiming at, make sure you add on your bonuses, car, health insurance, pension, gym membership – collect the monetary value of everything. You can then truthfully say what your total package is.

12. Hidden job market

We've covered using traditional methods of getting a job in Chapter 10, 'Making applications'; now it's time to perhaps step outside your comfort zone and try something new. It's time for you to take action.

You already know what you want; you can now make targeted contact with organizations. Of course, you aren't going to write to an organization, but to a relevant person within it, someone who may have the power to give you a job or to help you on your way to the job you seek.

Do not write to the HR manager unless you want to work in HR – HR is more concerned with screening people out.

Are you ready?

This is not the easy option, but you could well find it exhilarating, plus you are being active, not just reacting to jobs you see advertised. You are going to be focused and you are going to use psychology to help you. You will make connections with others to encourage them to support you.

What would make *you* want to help someone? An obvious mail shot? Or an approach by someone who has taken some time to understand more about who you are and what approach will be best to take? So you are not

Advert or recruiter appointed

HR takes over

Manager secures authorization

Job specification is written

The organization needs to recruit

The organization is aware of a problem that needs solving but does not think there is anyone within the organization who can help

going to fire off letters and messages indiscriminately but focus carefully on what you want and approach the right people.

Your letter will make it very clear **what you have to offer** – skills, experience, talents – and **who you are** (interests, values, personal style), plus the specific work area. You will not be vague! You will entice them to want to get in touch to find out more.

This is a sales letter that emphasizes accomplishments, not experiences, and is one or two sides long. As preparation you must identify the problems and challenges the organization faces and how you can help it increase sales or save money. This means that you do not focus on what you want – your goals and objectives – but on how you can help them. Your objective is to get a face-to-face interview.

Do not include your CV and if you are out of work, don't mention this.

To opt for this approach you need to be prepared for rejection. The average is a 4 per cent response rate – this means you have to send out 100 letters to get four positive responses on average, so be ready for rejection letters or no response at all.

Before the recession this really was an excellent way of getting a job, and it still can be. In the public sector it may prove difficult, as they have their processes and the direct approach can be frowned upon, so this is aimed more at people seeking a job in the private sector.

You need to prepare thoroughly, so here are the stages you need to go through.

Step 1: Online research
Step 2: Research the person
Step 3: Prepare your letters
Step 4: Send out your letters
Step 5: Follow up with a phone call
Step 6: At the meeting
Step 7: Follow up

Step 1: Online research

You know your strengths and the type of job you want. Now identify the type of organizations who are likely to have a need for someone like you. You also need to be clear on location – there is little point approaching organizations based in London if you need to live in Bristol and the job isn't flexible.

Research will focus both on current issues that you can use to target an approach and also relevant companies. You can identify organizations through:

- Suggestions from friends and colleagues.

- Reading newspapers and the trade press and looking online to see which organizations are growing, who is gaining government tenders, etc. You can also see which companies are advertising, maybe not in your field, but if they are taking on employees in one area, there may be other opportunities soon.

- Attending professional meetings, conferences, networking events, classes or workshops.

- Walking or driving around business and science parks to identify possible companies to approach.

- Working as a volunteer or serving on a committee.

- Participating in an online community, especially using LinkedIn.

- Contacting alumni of your university.

- Writing articles or public speaking relevant to your career.

- Market research online or in your local business library.

You can also buy lists of companies from Business Link. You can choose the location, industry, and size of company. Collating details into a spreadsheet will help you to keep track.

Step 2: Research the person

Once you have identified an organization you need to find the person to approach. This is likely to be the person who would be your boss. Do not send a letter or email without a person's name. If you have a background as a production manager, you would contact the production director. You can find out through looking on the company website, searching on LinkedIn or phoning and asking. It's probably worth checking via a phone call, as websites can be out of date.

Use your contacts, including people you are connected to through LinkedIn, to help. Ask people if they know anyone who works for the company you are going to contact. Then ask them if they will make an introduction.

 Once you identify an organization, use networking to find out the names of the appropriate head of department or decision-makers. Talk to people you know and see if they can introduce you.

Step 3: Prepare your letters

If you are looking for vacancies as a management accountant, there will be a lot of similarities between the letters you send to different organizations, but you still want a degree of personalization and your letter will differ if you are applying to a firm of architects or a light engineering company. You must target your letter to the particular organization.

The objective of the letter is not to get you a job but to get you seen by a decision-maker. Your letter has to be convincing and incisive. Demonstrate that you understand the organization's needs. Think about the problems that must be faced by the production director (or whoever) to whom you are writing. How can your combination of experience, training and aptitude help to deal with them? How can you make their life easier or more profitable?

This is a time-consuming approach, but you will have a much higher success rate if you tailor your letter specifically rather than take the mail-shot approach.

Below is an example of a poorly targeted approach. This is not focused on what the person can offer and is clearly a letter sent to many, setting the writer up for rejection.

Dear Sir/Madam,

I am writing to apply for a job as a **Business Development Manager**. I have a total of nine years of full-time work experience.

Attached is my detailed CV for your review. I would appreciate the opportunity to speak with a member of your recruiting team in due course.

I can be reached anytime via email at XXXXXX@hotmail.com or 07801 5xxxxx

Thank you very much for your consideration.

Sincerely,

To be successful with this approach, a letter has to grab attention, generate interest and desire, and provoke action. It should be focused on a particular job, not vague, saying something like 'I am writing in case you need someone with my qualifications and experience'.

Below are four key principles that you should aim to follow when creating your letters.

1. Aim to catch the reader's interest, to make them want to read the rest of your letter. For example, 'As an assistant marketing manager for a leading consumer product, I helped increase sales by 13 per cent through a new marketing policy.'

You want to show quickly how you can benefit the organization so don't start with the word 'I'.

2. Make a connection between what you can offer (in this first paragraph) and the needs of the organization, for example,

Your company may be in need of a sales consultant. If so, you may be interested in what I have achieved in sales.

Or

If your company needs a manufacturing manager with my background and experience, you may be interested in some of the things I have done.

Or

Do you have a need for a marketing manager? You may be interested in some of my accomplishments …

3. Include details of relevant achievements. Include the most relevant examples from your CV that highlight your key achievements that are relevant to the job you seek. Also mention your educational background, qualifications, etc. – these add credibility to what you are saying. Do not include anything which is not highly relevant for the job you seek. If possible, include numerical data to emphasize any achievements, just like on your CV.

4. End with the action required. Being proactive means being in control, so end your letter by saying what you will do next – phone in a few days. Don't say that you will wait to hear from them or you will be waiting forever. Far better to write something such as 'If you would like to discuss my experience in greater detail, I shall be glad to do so at a personal interview. I will phone you early next week.'

Also, it will not help your case if you write something like 'I would appreciate an opportunity to discuss any openings that you may have in your organization.' This weakens your position. You are selling yourself in your speciality.

I have not included model answers where you fill in the gaps as you are writing a document that influences and it has to reflect your own background and personality, but most importantly why you are approaching the organization and how you can help them. It should sound natural and be easy to read.

Once complete, read it out loud. Do the phrases come easy, or are the sentences so long that you run out of breath? Read it out loud to a friend or colleague and make sure they understand what you are trying to say.

Studies by the British Direct Mail Association show that a catchy PS can increase the response rate. What could you add? Perhaps something like 'P.S. I live close by and could call in and see you at short notice.'

Don't forget to add a reminder to your diary/calendar so you follow up with a phone call.

Use your research to create a mailing list of 300–1,000 people. You should aim to send out around 20 letters a week, and keep sending them out even as you move into a second interview phase. A job could fall through at the last stage and so you need to make sure that you won't have to start from scratch again.

 The direct approach is the most positive, the most effective, the most time-saving and the most reasonable way to get a job offer.

You generally want to send out a letter targeted to a particular company, showing you have done research and understand their particular needs, but sometimes you can send the same letter to a number of companies if like those below you are targetted on a specific job to a number of organisations.

Louise wanted to train as an accountant; through her research she identified the key skill requirements of accountants and structured her letter around the key competencies. She sent out 104 letters, resulting in five meetings and one job offer. The letter she used is below. It is a bit on the long side but it is an actual letter that worked!

Dear

Audit/Accounts Trainee

Recent analysis of my future career direction, including tests and discussions with an Occupational Psychologist, have indicated that training to be an accountant is the right next step for me. The reasons I believe I will be successful are:

Business understanding – Gained through a business studies degree and experience across a range of organizations such as XYZ Company. I have worked through periods of organizational change and so have first-hand experience of organizational challenges.

Motivation – Demonstrated motivation through the ability to study for a part-time degree alongside full-time work. I also set and focus on goals, and remain motivated despite

(continued)

---

challenges, such as my elderly father becoming seriously ill whilst working towards my exams. I passed with a merit.

Communication skills – I am used to producing reports and analysing data and have to explain complex issues to non-experts in an easy-to-understand way. My counselling qualification is evidence of my overall skills and I am noted for my ability to listen effectively to others.

Numerical skills – I enjoy using numerical data and am comfortable with interpreting figures.

Team skills – I am used to working effectively as a member of a team, and have contributed to effective teams where we each have our own areas of responsibility and knowledge.

Analytical skills – problem-solving is one of my strengths and I take a logical approach to analysing issues.

IT skills – Proficient across the Microsoft Office suite and very comfortable with the Internet, and use of email and in-house packages.

In every organization I have worked for I have been praised for my high level of attention to detail and customer-relations skills.

I appreciate that I am not a typical recent graduate, but believe I am a credible applicant due to my business degree and background, and the thought I have given to my future career direction.

(continued)

I already have gained the following four ACCA papers (by exemption): 1.1, 1.2, 1.3 and 2.2.

I have had exposure within a finance environment, totalling approximately nine months. This consisted of a placement within XYZ Credit Control department and a temporary assignment within Ambassador Financial Assurance.

I trust you find my details of interest and will telephone you in a few days to arrange a time to meet.

Yours sincerely

Louise Lawson (Enc: Curriculum Vitae)

And here is a second example that resulted in a six-month consultancy assignment:

Dear _____

Do you need expert guidance in supporting your educational marketing strategy? I can maintain and enhance your high profile through the use of the following attributes and skills:

- Excellent communication skills
- Strategic thinker
- Creative innovator

(continued)

- Self-motivated
- Able to work under pressure and to strict time schedules

I have an understanding of the key issues associated with further education plus over six years' management experience in marketing. Previously I was a sales manager in the IT industry.

The range of skills I can offer includes:

- Copywriting for publicity materials, leaflets, brochures, etc.
- Promotion incentives
- Public relations
- Market research
- New product development

Having spent time analysing my future career path with a career psychologist, I wish to utilize my marketing experience with my passion for further education. I understand the challenges to be how to effectively communicate with a wide audience (from 16 to over 60) and to encourage them to undertake formal study both full-time and part-time.

I would welcome an opportunity to discuss this with you and will call you on Thursday afternoon to arrange an appointment.

Yours sincerely

Simon Harvey

Step 5: Follow up with a phone call

Be proactive and follow up with a phone call. I suggest calling two days after the letter should have been received, so if the letter would be received on a Tuesday, follow up on a Thursday.

The phone will probably be answered by the recipient's assistant, so develop a rapport so that they want to help you. They may try to put you off, not know anything about your letter, suggest you contact HR – or they may have been primed by their boss and be expecting your call. Let's hope it's this last one, and it could be if your letter is powerful enough!

Many people want to avoid this step but you must pick up the phone!

The person you speak to may be skilled in the art of screening calls so if asked the purpose of your call, say you have written to xxx and are following up with a personal call. If they are unavailable, find out when would be a good time to ring.

A typical opening statement could be:

I wrote to Mr _____ on _____, suggesting a meeting. He should have received the letter yesterday. I'm phoning to arrange a suitable time.

My clients are often successful; they get positive replies for a number of reasons, including:

- The post has not yet been announced or passed on to a recruitment consultant to be filled.

- A vacancy has been announced but your letter has interested the company and once they have seen you, you have successfully jumped the early part of the recruitment process.

- Either your skills interest the organization because they are looking at new projects which require these, or your letter has led to the organization looking at new projects that require your particular abilities.

- The vacancy would have been filled by an internal candidate had you not written to the organization at that time.

Step 6: At the meeting

You've arranged to meet, so don't blow it. Make sure you plan effectively. Think about it from their point of view: you've raised their curiosity and there might be a possibility of an opening but they are likely to play it cool and to start off by telling you that there aren't any vacancies. Have questions planned but also be ready to answer any questions they may have.

Step 7: Follow up

Send a thank you note. The real purpose of this is not to thank them for spending time with you but to address the issues you discussed at the meeting. You went there to sell yourself, you asked searching questions, now follow up by demonstrating clear thought as to what was discussed. You can't prepare this in advance; you have to focus on what was discussed.

Send the letters again

You will not get to talk with everyone you wrote to, so send out a second letter about three weeks later. This will emphasize your seriousness to someone who was unsure of the purpose of your letter. Also, circumstances may have changed and they now have a possible need for you. This time your letter should start in a different way; think about what you can say that would encourage the reader to continue with your letter.

13. Interview preparation

Your CV can get you shortlisted, but you need to be able to perform well at interview to get the job. It may be a few years since your last interview, so it's worth starting your preparation now. You could get a call for an interview at any time. At the very least, you should be able to respond instantly to the following two questions:

1. Tell me about yourself

This or 'Talk me through your career to date' is likely to be the first question you are asked. The interviewer doesn't want a 20-minute ramble through everything you've done but focused highlights taking about a minute.

- Start with an introductory sentence to get the listener used to the tone of your voice, such as 'As you are aware ...' or 'Thanks for giving me the opportunity of an interview ...'

- Next provide a short summary of yourself and your achievements. This may differ depending on the particular job you are applying for.

- Follow with a brief chronology of your previous employment, concentrating on achievements and skills gained. You should spend more time on your most recent career and your key achievements, and less on the past. Focus on what is most relevant to the key aspects of the job you are applying for.

- Conclude with a strong statement emphasizing your abilities, and a question such as 'Would you like me to elaborate on any part of this?' or 'What more would you like me to tell you?'

2. Why do you want to work for us?

An employer wants you to show enthusiasm and conviction for this particular job. You need to explain how well you match up. Emphasize what you can contribute, rather than how the job will benefit you. Your response will be based on what you have learned about the company, so show that you have done your research. Explain what you have found and why it interests you.

Past behaviour is a good indicator of future performance, so you will be asked questions on what you have done, but they will also want to make sure that you have considered how you match up to the requirements of the job.

 Without the pressure of an interview, consider what you would say to the following questions:

- Why are you considering leaving XYZ Org?

- How did you get your position with XYZ Org?

- What have you been doing since you left XYZ Org?

- What are some of the things which you enjoyed doing at XYZ Org?

- What do you see as your greatest strengths as an employee?

- What have been your best achievements?

- What are the qualities needed in a good manager/engineer/accountant?

- What would be the area you feel least confident about if we offered you a job?

- How would your colleagues answer if we asked them about your faults?

- What do you feel you gained from your time with XYZ Org?

- How would your last boss describe you?

- What do you see yourself doing at ABC in five/ten/fifteen years' time?

- What led you to become an accountant/engineer/chemist?

- How did you spend your vacations from school/college/university?

- Tell me about your leisure interests.

- Why do you want this job?

- Why should we offer you this job?

- Are you considering any other jobs at present?

- What would be your reaction if we offered you the job, but at £XX,XXX p.a.? (Less than you hoped for)

You may also be asked some 'How would you ...' type questions. For example, if you are applying for a job as a marketing director, they will want to know your strategic ideas so you must do research in advance. A really good technique to use when faced with this type of question is to imagine you are working as a consultant and to talk the interviewer through the approach you would take. In that circumstance you would ask some questions and at the interview, if you need some information to help your thinking, don't be afraid to either ask the question or within your reply to say something like 'of course I would want to find out the answer to a couple of questions to enable me to tailor my suggestions'.

You will find that some interviewers still ask general questions; you need to treat these as if the interviewer had asked a specific question. For example:

How much do you know about ...
'I'm very familiar; just recently ...'

Or

What would you do if...
'I was faced with a similar situation last year. What happened was ...'

 Make sure you have thought through examples to many of the possible questions you could be asked.

Competency-based interview questions

Interviewers may opt for a competency-based interview. We've looked at how to answer these questions on application forms (see Chapter 10); you take the same approach at interview. As a psychologist, I was taught these techniques years ago – they are based on the premise that past experience is a good indicator of future performance.

You need to have a strategy to answer this type of question. You don't want to give vague answers. Use a structure to give clearer, more focused responses, such as the STAR approach (described in Chapter 10 in relation to making applications). Here's an example of a response that uses this method to address an employer's question.

Describe the **Situation** you were in: 'I didn't handle the transition to university well and failed my first-year exams.' This has to set the context and lead to the interviewer being interested in what you have to say.

What **Task** you were asked to accomplish: 'I knew that if I wanted to succeed, I had to develop better study habits and manage my time better.'

The **Actions** you took and why: 'I created a calendar and marked the due dates for all of my assignments and tests. Then I set aside certain hours each day for studying, allowing more for exam times.'

The **Results** of your actions: 'My essays were in on time, and I took notes regularly to make things easier for exams. Because I was separating study time from social time, I would work hard and then relax, which has helped my time management.'

Interview preparation

Start practising. You could use an interview coach, or you can role play with a friend who can ask you the questions. Don't just sit there and answer questions; try to experience the whole interview. Wear the clothes you would wear to an interview, knock on the door and wait to be asked to sit down.

Tell your friend that you want them to give you feedback on what you did well and how you can improve. Ask them to comment on your body language and tone; it's not just what you say but how you say it. You can also practise in front of a mirror, to see how your smile etc. comes across.

You can work through these questions alone, but always say your answers out loud, don't rely on what you hear in your head. (We always sound better in our head!) If you record your answers, you will be able to review how they sound, and you will notice the number of times you say 'you know' etc.

It can help to consider your answers from the perspective of the person who will be interviewing you. Think about what information they will want to hear. Think too of first impressions – judgements will be made of you from the moment they see you, so you need them to be as positive as possible.

As an interviewer, I expect my candidates to be well prepared. They will be ready with examples for most of the questions I ask and will ask me intelligent questions which demonstrate they have thought about the role and how they would be successful if they were offered the job.

Get yourself ready

Re-read your CV and cover letter or application, plus the job ad and any supporting information, and be 100 per cent certain you can back up every claim with a specific and detailed answer.

Think about any areas where you know you are weaker. What can you say to compensate for any perceived weakness? But also, you may have something extra that you can offer – experience of a particular situation such as dealing with exports to China, when you've read they've got their first order into this emerging market. This may be beneficial to your role so be sure to be ready to let them know.

By keeping up to date on news about the organization, you can be ready with some extra evidence to support your application. Most people fail to do this. Your preparation should go beyond what other candidates will do. Of course you will have looked at the company website, but be sure to have a view on its competitors and industry developments, and know what is happening right now through a news search in the business press and from comments on public sites.

You will gain a competitive edge if you can demonstrate your knowledge of the industry you are applying to, not just knowledge of the role you have applied for.

 Mental preparation
Just like a sportsperson, you must prepare mentally. Imagine every element of the interview and possible problems that you may be asked to address, and prepare a reply. This should include the emotional, feeling element. This will make it much easier for you to be effective on the day.

The personality of the interviewer

I do a lot of interviewing and notice the style of an individual interviewer can vary immensely. Using key personality theory:

Extroverts enjoy interviewing but can talk too much and may not be well prepared. You need to be clear about what you want to say, and as your interviewer takes a breath be ready to talk some more and provide an example. Whilst the more they talk the happier they are likely to be with a client, you do want to provide good evidence for them to refer to.

Introverts are less outgoing, more hesitant and take extensive notes so probably provide a lot less eye contact. You may find they don't follow up on all questions so be ready to provide more detail. Don't be put off by the lack of eye contact and don't expect them to smile.

Neurotic people tend to worry so can be wary and judgemental. They may be intimidated by those they consider more driven and intelligent than themselves. It may be hard to spot this with an interviewer, but if you think you are being interviewed by someone who is at a lower level than you, you may want to create a strong rapport at the start of the interview.

Stable people are warm, empathic and likeable. They understand that interviews can be stressful and stay calm and focused. Not much extra you need to do with someone like this, who is likely to bring out the best in you.

And don't forget, some people may style themselves on Jeremy Paxman and want to put you on the spot, and be very hard to impress.

REMEMBER THIS!!! The intelligent interviewer will ask discriminating questions, and those who are less bright will want to demonstrate their intelligence through asking clever questions.

REMEMBER THIS!!! As you prepare, you need to

- Re-read the job ad and review your CV and career history to be ready to answer questions and go into more detail on any topic.

- Find out the name(s) and position(s) of the interviewer(s); research the organization and the person/people who will be interviewing, as well as current and future business issues.

- Practise interview questions and prepare questions to ask (it's fine to have the questions you will ask written down).

- Be ready with a concise statement to explain why your previous employment ended or why you want to leave.

- Check the interview location so you know where it is and where you can park if you will be arriving by car.

- Plan what to wear, make sure your clothes are clean and you feel comfortable wearing them.

- Check for any breaking news that might impact on the company.

Think yourself to success at interview

As part of your preparation for interview, you will be practising interview questions, sorting out your interview clothes – but how much time do you spend on developing a positive attitude?

Does your inner talk say things like 'I probably won't get this, other people will be more qualified than me, I hate group discussions, find it hard to make an impact …'? These thoughts are likely to raise your anxiety level. You may find it better if you tell yourself:

- 'This is going to be a really interesting interview'
- 'I'm looking forward to talking about my experience'
- 'I want to learn more about the company'
- 'I will be fine regardless of whether I get the job or not'

This will help you be calmer and enable you to focus on your strengths.

It can be easy for negative thoughts to come into your head during the interview – 'I'm too old/too young for the job', 'I rambled through that answer', 'What if I don't get the job?' – but this distracts you from doing your best, so as these thoughts come into your head, blow them away! Take deep breaths and stay calm.

REMEMBER THIS!!! Don't get too excited about a forthcoming interview. Don't start dreaming that you already have the job and stop your job search. Keep looking as hard as ever until you get the contract. When you get an interview, always have another one lined up, including a fact-finding interview – it will stop you coming across as desperate.

Plan in advance to make a great first impression

We create an impression, either consciously or not. Erving Goffman, in his book *The Presentation of Self in Everyday Life*, discusses how we wear 'masks'; we change our expression to what is seen as appropriate for a particular situation. For example, the door-to-door sales person puts on a friendly expression as they walk up a path. We too should start smiling and look positive as we approach the building, not wait till we meet our interviewer. We can manage our impressions through the clothes we wear, the newspaper we read, and the pen we use. To provide a positive impression at interview we can dress similarly to the people who work in the organization we want to join, and to reinforce an image, carry a copy of a magazine – the *Economist* perhaps?

Think about the briefcase or bag you take and any pen and pad you may need to use: are these of good quality? Is this likely to be important? I once interviewed someone for a senior role and he brought along documents in a carrier bag – he was certainly making a statement!

Learn from the narcissists to ace the interview

Narcissism is a personality disorder where people have an inflated sense of their own self-importance and a lack of empathy. They are highly self-assured and confident and see themselves as superior to others, and at the same time can seek to put others down. Whilst many people may demonstrate these characteristics to some extent, only about 1 per cent of the population are suffering from this disorder.

A recent study from the University of Nebraska–Lincoln found that narcissists can be successful at a job interview; they aren't modest and are willing to talk about their strengths. They also appear enthusiastic and, according to the study, 'tend to dress a little nicer'.

So we can take some of these qualities and use them to our advantage. An interview is not the time for modesty; you must be clear on your strengths and be willing to give examples which demonstrate these strengths in an enthusiastic manner.

Over to you – questions to ask at the end of the interview

At the end of the interview, you will be asked if you have any questions. So many of the people I interview mumble about everything having been covered. It makes for a weak ending. The best candidates open their briefcase, pull out a pad with a few questions listed and choose three or four to ask, such as:

- Since the job was advertised, have your requirements been amended?

- Why are you going outside of the company?

- Who would I be replacing? Why is that person leaving?

- What would you see as my priorities in this job?

- If I were to be offered the job, what preparation could I do?

- I am very interested in this job and believe I can do it well; do you have any concerns about me as a candidate?

Your research will have identified why you will be a great candidate. Prepare a question you could ask at interview which would allow you to use a particular achievement as an illustration. You can do this for all of your strengths – this will mean you not only have great examples ready to use in answer to every question, but you can also ask questions of your own that reinforce your strengths. An example might be: 'Is there a need to simplify processes? I'm asking because when I was in my last job I introduced processing mapping, which resulted in savings of time and increased effectiveness.'

14. The interview

The previous chapter focused on preparation. This chapter takes you through what to do on the day of the interview to perform at your best.

When you arrive

Aim to arrive five to ten minutes early to allow time to check your appearance in the bathroom. Putting your phone on silent might be enough but as you don't want it to vibrate, it's probably best to play safe and switch it off. You may be kept waiting so bring something to read.

Be in a positive frame of mind. You may or may not feel confident but for the interview, you must portray a positive image. There's some research that says smiling can help make you feel happy. So put on a big smile and keep your eyes smiling afterwards.

Interviewers will often seek a general view on the candidates from administrators and so on, so be friendly and positive with everyone you meet. You know you will have to shake hands so have a firm handshake, and use antiperspirant if you have a tendency to sweaty hands.

At the interview

Many interviewers make up their minds about a candidate within seconds of meeting them. This is known as the 'halo effect'. When we observe one good thing about someone, we assume all kinds of other good things about the person. It's not fair, but we do it anyway. For example, if you are well dressed, many interviewers will assume you are probably responsible in other ways.

With the 'halo effect' the interviewer is subconsciously seeking to have that initial favourable impression confirmed by the subsequent discussion. The opposite is the 'horns effect'. If you start off badly, perhaps by the way you are dressed, your clammy hands or tripping up as you go into the interview room, you'll have an uphill struggle for the rest of the interview.

You can make the interviewer feel good right from the start. As you are greeted by them, you could say, 'I just want to let you know how much I appreciate you meeting with me. This position sounds so exciting and I've heard nothing but good things about [company name].'

Talent and experience are not enough; you need to come across as relaxed and enthusiastic. Expect to enjoy the interview and see yourself as an equal partner.

 You only have one chance to make a first impression.

Put into practice the techniques of relaxation and alertness. Make sure you breathe and listen. Be confident in your ability and how you will behave. Also be assertive: if, for example, you have the sun in your eyes, ask for the blinds to be dropped or to move your chair.

Use your body language to good effect: use hand gestures to emphasize a point – but not too much – and make eye contact. Too many people look shifty, as they don't want to look at the person interviewing them. If you find it hard to look directly at someone, imagine you are looking at a triangle made up of their eyes and nose.

Demonstrating confidence means that you will stand, sit, and walk with good posture and confidence. You will have a firm and decisive handshake, call the interviewer by his or her name, and say how pleased you are to be there (and mean it!).

Expect to get on with your interviewer, and show you do through your verbal and non-verbal behaviour. Younger people, and those who haven't been interviewed for a long time, in particular, can be nervous and emphasize a lack of confidence by a quiver in the voice and a shaky hand when picking up a glass of water.

Developing rapport

We discussed the importance of rapport in Chapter 5 ('Fact-finding interviews'). We are more favourable towards others when we are in rapport; salespeople know that techniques such as mirroring voice tone and posture work, and use them to make the sale. You need to use such techniques to help you perform well at interview.

Positive signs that you are in rapport include the interviewer smiling, leaning forward in their chair and nodding affirmatively. Negative signs include the interviewer frowning, checking their watch and not making eye contact with you.

Speak loudly and clearly enough to be heard. Make sure you stress your good points and show how well informed you are about the organization. Keep your attitude businesslike and respectful. Sell yourself by giving solid reasons why you want to work for the company and showing how you can help them.

Make sure you recount things in an interesting and positive way so that the interviewer will remember you. Listen closely as the interviewers introduce themselves. You should try to address them by name at some point during the interview.

Be natural, relaxed and enthusiastic. Remember, you are already more than halfway to the job. You are at interview because the selectors consider you can do the job. Unless you're a professional actor/actress, most employers will be able to see through any 'mask' you're trying to project. Be self-assured, but not over-confident, overbearing or arrogant.

Show your passion
If there are two equally qualified candidates, the more passionate one will likely get the job.

Think before you talk. Take a few seconds to collect and organize your thoughts, and then answer each question simply and directly. If you do not understand the question or the motivation behind it, ask for clarification. Use jargon or technical terms only if you fully understand them and if they will help to show your knowledge of a subject.

Facial expressions

Eye contact is important in communication. Research undertaken by the psychologist Michael Argyle emphasizes the importance of facial expression in communication. For example, if we want to know if the other person is interested, we can look into their eyes – our pupils dilate (get bigger) when we are aroused/interested. So that can encourage us in our communication. People will look at you more as they finish speaking, helping you to know that it is now your turn. If you look at someone while you are speaking you will appear more confident and sincere.

Answering questions

Before you start to answer a question, in your head say to yourself, 'Now I need to answer that question in a way that will show how I can be of value to this employer.' If you start to ramble, interrupt yourself by coughing or pausing. This will give you time to collect your thoughts and you can say 'Sorry, can I start that answer again?'

As you cover them at interview, mentally tick off the five or six key reasons why you should be considered for the job. Find opportunities to raise any topics which have not been covered. You might be asked whether you would like to add anything or you might make the point yourself: 'Would it be helpful if I mentioned something else relevant to this job?' Take every opportunity to explain your achievements and abilities within the context of the job description.

Never hesitate to ask the interviewer to repeat the question if you haven't fully heard or understood it. You can also use the technique of restating the question in different words to check your understanding.

Let the interviewer control the interview, but always be prepared to take the initiative. Have a strategy for handling interviewers who monopolize the talking, or ask only closed ('Yes/No') questions. Be prepared for the deliberate question which the interviewer knows you cannot answer. Such questions are useful to interviewers as much to see how you will cope as for the content of your reply.

If the interviewer starts asking questions where you need to imagine yourself in the role, for example, asking you 'How would you handle ...?' it is very helpful to pretend that you are not being interviewed for a job. Instead, imagine that you are a respected consultant helping a new client with a problem. Adopt a probing approach so that you can understand their situation in sufficient detail before providing an answer. Relate your answer to their business objectives rather than to theories or models (unless specifically asked to do so).

Similarly, when asked about your past achievements, relate them to issues your employer was trying to address and the business (organizational) benefits they gained. This way, you will be giving very useful examples, and, by not trying to 'perform', you will be more relaxed.

- **Keep on your toes.** Everyone feels nervous before an interview; this is quite natural. Butterflies in the stomach are caused by the same surge of adrenaline that an athlete gets before an important race. It's the body's way of tuning up your faculties for peak performance. Channel this energy by keeping super-alert and notice the interviewer's body language for clues on how much detail you should be giving them. For example, do they appear attentive or bored?

- **Build rapport.** The interview is also about what you are like to work with. Hence, building rapport may be as important as impressing with expertise.

- **Give careful consideration to all your answers.** Don't be afraid to pause and think before replying to a question, and don't hesitate to say you don't know if that is the case (but not too often!).

- **Be natural.** Wanting to give your best doesn't mean that you have to be unnatural. High anxiety about the outcome can lead to candidates either trying too hard or coming over as dull and stilted. Aim to strike a balance between being (a) comfortable and relaxed and (b) alert and incisive. Above all, show your interest by your natural enthusiasm for that winning future combination – you and the job.

- **Be positive.** Handle mistakes properly. Don't criticize previous employers, as you'll project a negative image of yourself. On the other hand, if you have made a mistake in your career, it is not a disaster to admit it, but make sure you convey clearly the lessons it taught you. Admitting the odd mistake also gives you credibility when you start to talk about the positive things in your career.

Your questions

You will have prepared your questions; you may like to use some of the ones listed in the previous chapter. Open your folder and read them out. You must include a question to identify some of the organization's problems. You can then focus your thank you letter on addressing these issues.

A perfect close

Once you have asked your questions, you have a final chance to make a positive impression. You can now make a one-minute closing statement. Summarize your qualifications, skills and accomplishments and emphasize your interest in the job. Thank the interviewer, and be sure to ask about the next step or stage. Make sure you say goodbye to the receptionist as you leave.

Post-interview evaluation

Once you are out of the building, and in your car or at the train station, jot down a few notes, outlining the main points discussed.

As soon as you can, complete a review of how you think you came across. It will be invaluable to refer to if you get a second interview and you can also use it to monitor your performance. Be honest with yourself, noting what you did well, and where improvements are needed. Talk through the result of your review with a friend and practise your revised answers.

There are many questions you can ask yourself, such as:

- Was I in the right frame of mind?

- Was my eye contact right? Did I smile?

- Was there anything I should have known about the company that I did not?

- How effective was my role in the interview?

- Which questions did I handle well? Which questions did I handle poorly?

- How well did I ask questions? What could I have done differently?

- Did I appear confident and show genuine enthusiasm?

- Did I talk too much?

- Did I give answers which didn't seem to satisfy the interviewer?

- Was I able to discuss my strengths and weaknesses?

- Did I find out all I needed to?

- Would I like to work for that organization?

 Give yourself a reward after the interview – perhaps a nice lunch or your favourite coffee and cake!

Contacting the recruitment agency

If you have been put forward by a recruitment agency, call them as soon as you can to enthusiastically let them know how you got on and to confirm your interest in the job. They will almost certainly feed this straight back to the interviewer and it will be viewed positively.

Follow up with a thank you letter

Very few candidates write a follow-up letter. If the interviewer is still deciding between you and another candidate, this may just tip the balance in your favour.

The purpose of your thank you letter is to reinforce your strengths, experience and accomplishments. Include anything that relates to and expands on what was discussed at interview. It is not just to thank them for their time.

Your thank you letter can address areas of weakness, and any reservations or concerns that were mentioned during the interview. You can also explain how your strengths and past work history (with examples) can over-compensate for any areas of weakness.

Most importantly, you will provide brief details of how you can solve the recruiter's problem. But you don't want to tell them everything – you want them to get back in touch with you.

A sample letter:

Thank you for the opportunity to interview with you last Tuesday for the position of Business Development Manager. During the interview you asked why I was a good candidate and I could only give you a vague response. I have spent time evaluating my strengths in relation to your needs. After serious consideration I can comfortably state that I am a good candidate because _____.

You also said that one of the problems you have is XXX, I've been thinking of ways to solve this and would love an opportunity to discuss my ideas further. I have identified one area in particular …' and then you explain how you could solve this problem. You should aim to explain what you would do, but not how you would do it, that's what you want to discuss with them at a second interview.

Hold back some key details though – you don't want to give everything away; you want them to call you back for a further interview.

Second and third interviews

You will need to do some extra research for subsequent interviews, but don't forget to review your notes from the first interview. The more knowledgeable you are in advance, the more effective you will be. Remember that everyone you meet, from division head to support staff, is evaluating you, just as you are evaluating them. Always ask about the next steps after the interview and when you will hear from them. Then make a diary note to get in touch the day after.

What to do if you don't get the job

If you are offered the job you still need to make sure it is the right job for you and Chapter 17 will be useful. But you may get a rejection letter.

In some cases it will be what you expected. In your post-interview review, you will have identified where you could have done better, and can use this learning for next time. In other cases you may not be able to identify anything wrong. You may have done a brilliant interview and still not have been offered the job.

It could be that there was more than one person who was capable of doing the job and the final decision may have been based on factors outside your control. The person who got the job may have been an internal candidate or had something extra to offer. Or there may never have been a job available. The head office may have wanted to fill the vacancy but the job had already been offered to someone, and the whole interview process was a sham.

Whatever you think is the reason you didn't get the job, contact the organization and ask for feedback.

Finally, even if you do not get an offer, you can still write one last letter. The person who has been offered the job may turn it down. Quite regularly, a new employee leaves fairly quickly as it hasn't worked out for them. Your letter could bring you to the top of the list when a new person is being considered.

15. Phone and Skype interviews

Many companies conduct phone interviews at the first stage of shortlisting.

You should expect to get phone interviews, so be prepared: you should sound energetic and upbeat, both when you talk and via your answerphone message – so make sure on both your landline and mobile you have a clear and businesslike message such as:

Hello, this is (your name). I'm sorry I'm not available to take your call right now. Please leave your name, phone number, a brief message, and the best time to reach you. I'll get back to you as soon as possible.

Most people project themselves much better over the phone when they are standing up, so get on your feet. (Try it with a friend or family member and see if they notice the difference.)

Often a time will be scheduled for the call, and you may be sent information on the job to help you to prepare. Other times you may be phoned by a recruiter who wants to conduct the interview there and then. In this case you are unlikely to be prepared, so tell the caller you are about to leave for the dentist and agree an alternative time. This means you will be prepared and in a 'peak state' for the phone interview.

The call could come through when you are in a noisy environment; far better to arrange to talk later than to struggle when it's hard to concentrate and to miss out on some of the questions asked. Background noise may irritate both you and the interviewer. Have a quiet room you can go to so that neither you nor the caller is going to be distracted.

Your voice is key, so be aware of how you sound. Record yourself talking and listen. Do you sound enthusiastic? Do you speak clearly? Remember, the person on the other end of the phone won't pick up on your smiles and nods so you need to convey interest with carefully chosen words and appropriate voice inflections. The phone artificially speeds up sound, so speak slightly slower than usual. It can also depress the sound of your voice, so put some variety into your speech.

You can have material to refer to spread out in front of you, but you need to be able to manage the documents – you don't want the recruiter to hear you flicking through papers for your answer. Some people like to use index cards with possible questions and details of skills, abilities and other strengths written on one side and examples on the reverse.

The call usually starts with confirming factual information and then asking more specific questions, often related to key competencies and characteristics of the job. In a screening call they are confirming the detail in your CV.

Make sure you make a note of the person's name so you can refer to them by name.

Typical questions

The first question may be 'Is it okay if I record your responses?' If they are going to do this, they may stop and check recording levels, so be patient. You may be asked for a brief overview of your career. Say exactly the same things you would say at a face-to-face interview. Prepare and practise this until it comes naturally to you.

Some recruitment consultants use a short psychometric test, often giving you four options of characteristics from which you have to choose the one which is most like you and the one which is least like you. Don't try to second-guess what they are looking for, just come across as a positive version of yourself. You may be asked for specific examples against the competencies. These are the areas you would prepare for at a face-to-face interview, so get your preparation done ahead of time.

 Practice call
A practice phone interview with a friend or coach can help improve your confidence and technique. Often when nervous, we waffle. So get feedback on how you come across.

Skype interviews

Just a few years ago, video conferencing involved using expensive equipment. Now it is much easier through the use of Skype. Maybe you already use Skype to talk with friends. It's free to download and all you need is a webcam, a microphone and an internet connection. Skype makes it easy to be interviewed for work when it would not be practical for you to travel, and is being used more and more for first interviews.

If you have never used Skype before, set up a few video calls with friends or family.

Adjust the settings to ensure that you are clearly in shot, and make sure you don't set the zoom too high – your face shouldn't fill the screen; have some background as well.

The background should be neutral; you don't want the interviewer to be distracted by the objects in your room. Think about lighting – they need to be able to see you, so close the curtains if it is too sunny and have the lights on if the room is dark. Test the technology to make sure you are heard. Just as with your email address, make sure you have a professional Skype name.

Make the video of your interviewer full-screen so that you are not distracted by anything else on your computer. Turn off any sounds or notifications that might pop up in the background. Turn off your mobile phone and ensure family and pets will not disturb you.

Check how you look on the screen and make adjustments to the camera angle. If you use a laptop, place it on a stable surface rather than have it wobbling on your knees. Wear business clothes, and not just on your top half – you may need to stand up! Look at the camera rather than the screen to help give the appearance of eye contact.

Prepare to the same extent as you would for an in-person meeting. Have pen and paper ready so you can make notes but be cautious when referring to your notes; each time you look at them you are not looking at the camera.

 You could have key points written on Post-it notes on the side of your screen.

16. Staying motivated

No matter how positive a person you usually are, when job hunting, particularly if the need for a job is urgent, it can be hard to keep your spirits up. Let's look at some action you can take to keep going.

Dealing with rejection

You will get setbacks and knockbacks, so you need to be ready for them. When we don't get shortlisted it is not personal: many times it has been done by a computer system; at interview there can be many people who could do the job equally well.

What we can do is to review everything we are doing to see if there are any ways we can improve. We may think we have a great CV, but if it is not getting us to interview, it is not doing its job. So keep track of your rejection letters and if necessary seek an independent job-search coach to provide feedback and guidance to help you improve.

It may be that you need to create a more focused CV and cover letter, or you may need to spend more time on research – re-read the advice in this book.

You may think you interview well, but carrying out a full interview with an experienced interviewer who coaches you is worth the investment. The relevant chapters in this book tell you how to conduct yourself at interview, and practice sessions with a friend may help you improve, but you may still benefit from exploring other subtleties with an experienced interviewer.

Keep a positive attitude

Whether you think you can or you can't, you're right.

Henry Ford

You need a positive attitude: you need to believe that you can do something, that you can achieve your goal. You could find inspiration through books and reading other people's success stories – for example, there is a Facebook group, AmazingPeopleUK, where clients of my Amazing People company share good news and get energized and inspired through reading what others have done.

Use much more positive self-talk. Before an interview you can say things like, 'My body is relaxed and I feel confident.' During an interview you can say to yourself, 'I'm calm and in control, I'm speaking clearly and have great examples to share.' After an interview you can say, 'I'm doing well, I've learnt more about interviews to help me for next time.' While you wait to hear the outcome of an interview you can say, 'I am a worthwhile person and the right job is out there.'

Negative self-talk can really hamper our chance of a new job. If we ask ourselves, 'Why can't I get a job?' our brains will focus on all the reasons why we can't get one – we are too old or too young, too fat or too short, have too much experience or not enough. We need to get our subconscious minds working on a different question, something like 'What can I do to get this job?' or 'How can I show an employer that I'm the right person for this job?'

Stop saying 'I can't get a job'; change it to 'I will get a job'. Stop saying you are useless and remind yourself that you are doing something useful each day. Don't say you are too old (or too young) but that you are the right age for a new opportunity. Don't say you don't want to be unemployed and instead say, 'I'm excited about getting a new job.'

Instead of worrying about not knowing where to start, you can say, 'I'm ready to get started', and let your subconscious work on this.

If we expect to be unsuccessful in meetings and at interview, then we are likely to come across that way, and will be seen as someone who can't confidently discuss the great examples of their experience. However, if we think we are going to be successful and have planned how to respond to and ask questions, we stand a much better chance.

The need for confidence

Confidence means that we have the belief that we will succeed. When we lack confidence, we set ourselves up for a negative and downward spiral. When we lack confidence, we don't perform well, which is less likely to achieve success and will reduce our levels of confidence still further.

Lacking confidence means that our performance is more hesitant, and less likely to be successful, so we don't get the job, which affects our confidence still further.

Our thought processes

What we think can have a powerful impact on our confidence. If we have negative thoughts and beliefs it can result in a downward spiral. Check yourself and see how many times you hear the following voices in your head. You may hear:

The Critic who tells you what a disappointment you are and that if you ask for help it is a sign of weakness.

The Perfectionist who tells you that you should do this and you must do that, and that you have to be perfect in everything you do, and that you must be competent at all times – it is unthinkable to fail.

The Worrier who gets you to catastrophize and ask 'What if ...?' questions, such as 'What if I don't get this job?'. Maybe you won't, but you should learn from it and improve for next time. Catastrophizing and expecting the worst doesn't help; you need to focus more on performing well.

The Victim who knows that it is nothing to do with them, it's all to do with someone else. They think that nothing will make any difference and expect to fail at the interview, will tell you that no one wants you and that you will never be able to get another job.

We must challenge these voices. We mustn't let these voices take over. Stop saying 'No one ever responds to my job applications' – really? No one? Stop thinking that people are out to get you. Many people apply for jobs and not getting shortlisted can be down to many reasons outside your control.

We need to hear different voices, the ones that tell us that we are on track and to focus much more on the positive. Instead of thinking of disappointments we need to think of our successes and remind ourselves of situations we handled well, times when people praised and thanked us, and so on.

It's not just the voices in your head

Does your family get you down?

Does your partner, or do your parents, continually ask you when you are going to get a job? One way to keep them 'off your back' is to set up a weekly review time so you can show what you have done and what you plan to do for the subsequent week. Tell them how their nagging isn't helping, and recruit them to be part of your network, assisting you in finding leads and people to talk with.

Are your friends helping?

Some people love to be negative, to see the world as a half-empty glass, to complain, to see problems, to expect to fail. Spend too much time with people like this and you are likely to start thinking the same way. Who do you know that will inspire you and keep you feeling positive? You need to spend more time with people like that! Perhaps you should look to broaden the circle of people you know and meet more positive people. Perhaps joining a book group or a walking group would help. Find out details of groups local to you through Meetup.com.

Switch off the news

If each day you watch programmes about how awful the job market is, how many people are being made redundant and so on, you may wonder how you will ever find a job yourself. Remember, you are not trying to get a job for everyone – just one job, for you.

Let's be more positive

Visualize yourself succeeding

Imagine yourself being successful in your job search – it can be a very powerful technique. Think of how you will dress and what the workplace will be like. Imagine yourself at your desk and on the phone, talking with customers or in the field delivering goods and services.

Maybe the image isn't clear at the moment, but try to picture yourself carrying out your ideal job – what will you be wearing? How will you be feeling? What will you do?

Successful athletes dream about winning. They visualize themselves achieving their goal. You can do the same! Each evening when you go to bed, make a movie in your head of being in your ideal job. What do you see? What can you hear? What can you taste or smell? Notice how great you feel! Run this movie through your head again – make it bigger, brighter and sharper. It works for athletes, and can work for you too.

Remind yourself of previous successes

Can you remember a time when you won a race, created a great report, made a presentation that convinced your boss to go ahead with a project or to give you a rise? Now is the time to remind yourself of previous successes. You might like to buy a small notebook and write them down as you remember them. You've been successful before and you will be again.

 Re-read your CV each day to remind yourself of your achievements and what a great job you did.

Remind yourself that it's not all within your control

You can have a great CV, interview well and look great but still find yourself unemployed and waiting for a job offer. Many people find themselves in this position – even more in times of recession. So keep doing the best you can and don't take your lack of a job offer too personally. Not getting a job does not mean that you are not a wonderful person, and you should look for as many ways as you can to keep your spirits high.

Think of the upside

I don't want to negate how people feel if they are so short of money they think they will lose their home, but for some people having more free time means they could do something they have never had time to do before, such as learning a foreign language, or getting fitter with a daily brisk walk or run.

The impact on others

Feel sorry for yourself and you will feel like a victim; spend too much time moaning and people won't want to be around you. Look for ways to remain interesting and to keep friendships and relationships going.

 You can't be in a happy and an unhappy mood at the same time. Changing your posture and facial expression can help. Put on a happy face and keep saying, 'I feel happy, I feel healthy, and I feel terrific.'

What might help?

Quit, just for a while

If you are getting down, you could give yourself a job search holiday: take some time out and take your CV down from all the job sites. Check that you still want to aim for the job you have been seeking. Get someone to provide a critical review of your CV, make any changes, and then start afresh.

Connect with more people

Of course you will be talking with people who have a high probability of helping you reach your job-hunting goals but sometimes doing something less focused on your job search leads to success. Perhaps talking with a neighbour and spending time listening to them could be helpful in both building your community and directing you to helpful contacts.

Develop new skills

Learn something that will enhance your CV. It doesn't have to be an expensive course; there are lots of training opportunities available for free. For example, you can access online training via the Massachusetts Institute of Technology online site at ocw.mit.edu. You may not be able to gain a qualification but you can still learn new skills. How can you improve – what can you do today to make a difference?

Volunteer

Could you use some of your spare time in voluntary work? You could use the skills you already have to benefit others, or use this as an opportunity to develop new skills. You may meet people in a position to offer you a job. At the very least, you will meet people who you can add to your network. And remember, many prospective employers think highly of a person who is involved with volunteer activities, so it will enhance your CV.

 The best volunteering when you are job hunting involves doing something related to the job you seek. If you are a marketing executive, offer to create a marketing plan for a charity. This will be far more effective for your job search than volunteering to work in a charity shop or tidying a country park.

Get a job search buddy
You may find your job search more fun with a buddy, who you can meet on a weekly basis to share progress. Find someone else in a similar situation to you who will help keep you motivated and with whom you can share ideas.

17. The job offer

Getting a job offer is excellent news – it's what you have been working towards. However, just because you get an offer, it doesn't mean you should say yes. Your interview can be a good indicator of how you are going to be treated in the job. James was extremely pleased to be shortlisted for a job with an accountancy firm. The interview with the HR manager went well but when he met his potential boss, he was rude and offhand.

If you hear people making negative comments about an organization or realize the job is a poor fit, think twice before saying yes. One of the worst things you can do is take a job and within a couple of weeks realize you made the wrong choice. You then have to spend time learning your new job, leaving even less time to restart your job search. Or you may resign and have a problem explaining to a new employer why you left so quickly.

Before you say yes

Send a letter to show your enthusiasm for the job. Remind them why they have chosen you. This letter should summarize your strengths, and outline your key accomplishments and personal contributions.

If the employer's compensation package has been outlined, say how excited you are and that you would like a couple of days to discuss things with your partner. This gives you a chance to weigh the pros and cons of the job, and to get in touch with any other organizations with which you have outstanding applications.

Gill was very pleased to be offered a job as marketing manager for an international company. It came with a substantial pay rise, international business-class travel and an executive car, and most people she knows would see this as a brilliant job. But when we discussed this job offer she realized that all these things weren't as important to her as spending time with her new husband and being able to work as a charity fundraiser, her ideal job.

It's worth taking some time to consider how important the following are to you; you can then compare job offers against these factors. Before saying yes, ask yourself:

- Is there a high possibility of security of employment?

- Will this job make good use of my abilities, skills and talents?

- Does it suit my personality?

- Am I happy that I will be paid fairly for the work I'll do?

- Am I happy with the salary/bonus aspect of my compensation package?

- Does the working environment suit my values and personal preferences?

- Will it give me a chance to develop and grow?

- Is the travel-to-work distance acceptable?

- Does my manager have the right approach to bring out the best in me?

- Am I likely to enjoy working with my customers/colleagues?

- What impact will taking this job have on my personal and family life?

- Is there a possibility of promotion (if this is important to you)?

- Are the expectations on me realistic and achievable?

- Why specifically do I want to take this job?

- How well does it match my ideal job?

Finalize the details

Before saying yes, make sure you also know the answers to these questions:

- What is my job title?

- To whom do I report? You could ask to meet the person at this point if you haven't already.

- Who will report to me?

- Am I clear on the duties expected of me? Do I have a full copy of the job description?

- Are the limits of my authority clearly defined?

- What are the hours of work?

- What are the sick pay entitlements?

- What are the holiday entitlements?

- Will any pre-booked holidays be honoured?

- How long will it take me to get to work and back each day at rush hour, and how much will this cost?

We spend the majority of our time in work, so arrange to talk with other employees to get an inside perspective. These could be your new manager and colleagues.

Saying no

Some people will think it foolish to turn down a job, especially in times of recession or when the job market is stagnant, but if it isn't providing what is important to you (you are being asked to work too many hours, thus creating a very low hourly wage, or you're not sure you'll enjoy the work as much as you'd like), then you may be better off waiting for a job that's more appealing.

Make sure you have considered *everything* the job offers, including the salary. It may be better to get 75 per cent of what you ideally want than continue for another six months being unemployed.

If you decide to turn an offer down, do so quickly and send a letter which keeps open the possibility of your getting in touch again in the future. For example:

Thank you for offering me a position as a Marketing Executive with Guardian Consulting. I found our discussions during the interview process very enlightening as to the details of this position, and I appreciate the time you allowed me to consider your offer. I was also able to confirm my initial impressions of Guardian Consulting as an outstanding organization.

However, after considerable thought about my career goals, I'm afraid I must respectfully decline your kind offer. I have chosen to accept an offer from an employer based closer to my home. This was a difficult decision for me, although I believe it is the appropriate one at this point in my career.

I want to thank you for the time and consideration you have given my application. It was a pleasure meeting you and learning more about Guardian Consulting.

Finally

If you accept the job offer, go back to every site where you have uploaded your CV and have it taken off. You won't want your new boss to see you still have your CV up there; it may make them think you are looking for another job.

Index

Notes

You can use the following pages to make your own notes on any of the exercises in the book.

Notes

Notes

Notes

Notes

Notes

Notes

Notes

Notes

Notes